Twisted Hair
And
The People of One Fire

Holly Sullivan McClure

Lost Mountain Press

©LMP 2018
Published by Lost Mountain Press 2018

This is a work of fiction based on legends and historical
events of the Indigenous people of North America.

Author: Holly Sullivan McClure

Interior artwork: Tim Nuttle

Revised edition

978-0-9982279-0-0

Acknowledgment:

The symbol of the fire was designed by Tim Nuttle. It is composed of overlapping flames of words in Cherokee syllabary letters. The foundation of the fire (Wajila) is the mound of Gadugi, service provided by the community. When we dance around the sacred fire at the ceremonial ground, it is done in an honorable, respectful way. This

brings medicine to the people. This is beautiful [uwodi] and I like that (agilvkwdi). These words are inseparable and interlinked, as are the concepts they attempt to communicate.

To obtain a signed print of this artwork, contact the artist at nuttle.tim@gmail.com**.**

Dedicated to the One Fire People who even now stand as protectors of the earth. And to the storytellers who keep the memories alive and pass them on to the next generation.

Introduction:

I listened to the elders tell their stories and hung on every word. I believed, because they believed. Animals spoke to people, guardian beings walked among us, the invisible, immortal Nunne'hi lived beside us in lands beyond hidden portals. Everybody knew someone who had seen them, perhaps even entered their world. When storytellers pointed out landmarks where events in the legends occurred, it removed any shred of doubt.

11,000 years of history linked the Cherokee people to the mountains and rivers of the homeland. Perhaps it's that history that draws me back. Long after the grandparents and relatives I used to visit are gone, I return and feel at home. The longing to stand in the *mother town*, the first home of the ancestors, where the **Keetoowah** lived, and the sacred fire burned, was part of my consciousness from earliest childhood. Thousands of years, it stood in the bend of the river, a place of pilgrimage, where the wisdom keepers preserved the stories, songs, and sacred ways for generations yet to come. Holy people kept the fire of unity and harmony alive. A few embers carried home, took the essence of that sacred place to other towns and united them as one people.

I couldn't visit the *mother town*. No one knew where to find the first home of the Cherokee people. It fell to outsiders who destroyed it and scattered the Keetoowah. With the removal and Trail of Tears, the location faded from memory and only the story and the yearning for home remained.

A field beside a heavily traveled highway yielded the first clue with the discovery of ancient bones. Evidence of habitation emerged, and archaeology proved the legends.

Now, the Eastern Band Cherokee own the site and it is possible to make that pilgrimage and stand on the mound where the sacred fire burned.

I wrote **Twisted Hair** before I knew the location of the mother town. I had only the memories of the stories, told at night around the fire, to fuel my imagination, but the town came to life in those stories. Standing on the mound, kindling my own fire on the site of the ancient sacred fire, completed a circle for me.

I used the three legendary holy men who traveled the land, observing, learning, and holding the knowledge, stories, wisdom and sacred ways that kept the people strong, to tell the story of the legendary holy man, Twisted Hair and the People of the One Fire.

Twisted Hair

Going Home

A snarling war dog caught the scent of the small band escaping into the cover of the jungle. The war chief's wife clutched her infant son against her breast and urged her daughters to run faster. Twisted Hair sent the boy he called Tsi-s-qua, to guide the women while he faded back to stand with the warriors and face the dog. It closed in. Fiercer than any wolf, trained by the strangers to attack and devour, he bared his teeth and hurled the full force of his fury at his closest adversary. With his only weapon, the great staff of the storyteller, Twisted Hair parried the attack. The war chief caught the vicious beast on his spear, eliminating the lesser threat to his family.

The war chief retrieved his spear. He indicated two warriors with its tip and gave them orders. "Protect my family and the holy man."

With a nod, the two raced down the trail behind the woman.

The chief reached to touch the great staff, tracing with his palm the feathered serpent that snaked its way among carved symbols of the people. "Don't let our story die with us."

Like shadows, he and his men vanished back through the jungle, returning to a hopeless battle against strangers who came from the sea, wearing armor like shining turtle shells and killing without mercy.

Thunder of strange weapons and howling of war dogs faded with distance. Twisted Hair and Tsi-s-qua took the lead, breaking a path for the woman and her children. The two warriors trusted with their defense, brought up the rear.

A narrow path intersected their course. Little used and forgotten by most, it snaked through the undergrowth. Here, the woman and her children must go on alone with only the two warriors to protect them.

She pleaded with Twisted Hair and Tsi-s-qua "Come with us where you will be safe. My brother's people have many strong warriors. They will help us."

"Warriors cannot protect us now," Twisted Hair said. "They are powerless against these strangers who come from the sea. Go to your brother and tell him to remember the stories of the elders. The wise will understand."

He and the boy watched the war chief's family and the two warriors until they vanished among the thick flora that flanked the trail.

They set out alone, making their way through marshland and saw-grass that tore at their leggings, traveling inland on a journey to the only place that offered a faint ray of hope. The sole chance for rescue from the new evil that threatened their people lay far away in the mountains covered with smoke.

Through great mound cities along the waterways they traveled, taking no time to rest. When Twisted Hair warned the people of the approaching peril, they assured him they feared no enemy. Their strong warriors stood at the ready to meet any threat.

He learned to keep silent and wait.

Beyond the waterways, they passed through scattered towns and villages in the hills and plains. With a wary eye on the trail behind him, Twisted Hair rose when dawn first touched the morning and kept going until light faded from the sky. North, then west, he trudged, spurred on by dread of what lay behind and hope that an answer waited in the distant mountains.

He took brief respite in towns where people welcomed him with rejoicing and offered him the best of all they possessed. The warmth of their welcome faded when they sensed the fear he tried to hide.

The wise were not deceived.

At night, he fought off fatigue and sat at the fire with the elders, telling stories the ancestors passed down through generations of wisdom keepers.

"Wrapped in myths and legends lie the mysteries and sacred ways of our people," he said. "When you keep the stories alive, the children's children will remember the heritage of strong nations and holy teachings. I entrust them to your keeping. Teach them to the next generation as I have taught them to you. I will not pass this way again."

He watched dismay settle over the people like an icy rain but said nothing to reassure them. Their fear gave him a measure of encouragement. Perhaps it would make them more vigilant. If they prepared for danger, a few of them might endure.

In every town where he lodged, the wisest stayed awake and lingered around the fire after most went to their lodges to sleep. They implored Twisted Hair to tell them more about the mysteries concealed within the stories, to bring to their memory the old ones who sang the songs and knew the earliest days of their people. He drew comfort from this. To the sagest elders and the wisest of the young, he revealed his dread and hinted at its source. A prophecy was fulfilled, the desolation it anticipated drew nearer every day, and nothing they could do would turn it aside.

His dread infected them, but he saw courage too. The

spirit of the people was strong. They would not forget the wisdom of the ancestors. He recalled stories of great men and women who came before and watched the people draw strength from the revered old ones.

As soon as dawn lit the sky, he and Tsi-s-qua took up their packs and departed on their long and weary journey, leaving their hosts with a final warning of approaching peril. He said farewell to old friends, knowing this parting marked a transition from ways that sustained the people. Dark days lay ahead, and he would not be there to guide them through the shadows.

They knew it too. He heard it in their voices as they sent him on his way. They gave him supplies packed on travois with strong dogs to convey them. It made the way easier.

In every village, they stayed long enough to implore the people to keep the stories in their hearts and teach them to the children. Twisted Hair saw his fear reflected in their eyes. When they promised not to forget the sacred ways and the stories that teach them, he took up his staff and walked away. There was nothing more he could do.

Late at night, when they thought he slept, he heard them whisper about the secret they saw behind his eyes that caused him to be afraid.

"What has he to fear?" they said. "The Twisted Hair can walk throughout the land in safety. No one would harm the holy man, yet he looks back at the trail he has traveled like a man who flees an enemy."

What if he told them how close they came to the truth, would they listen? Would it make them lose all hope to know the foe he fled brought the end of the world they knew?

He kept his own council and watched fear invade the

hearts of the wise in every village. In the evening, when their songs fell silent and dancing feet were still, even the smallest children sensed something wrong. They left their play and clustered around the mothers.

Tsi-s-qua sat with the elders, listening. Twisted Hair watched and was pleased, remembering nights he sat at the feet of the old storyteller, learning the stories, sacred ways, and tales of strangers who would come from the sea.

When he prepared to leave them after only a day or two, the people didn't understand why he had to go. They expected him to linger as he did in the past, to rest from his journey and teach them what he learned from storytellers in other towns along his trail. In past visits, he brought new stories, and news from faraway places, even a few trade goods, but not this time. He traveled with the boy and three pack dogs, asking for more stories than he told, reminding the people of the wisdom and sacred ways that lay at the center of the legends, insisting they remember. Then he replenished his pack with supplies for a journey and hastened back to the trail.

In every town, the elders wondered what brought such deep suffering to his eyes, and why he stayed no more than a night or two then departed in early morning. At first light, he turned back to his journey and gave them no answer. It would do no good to tell them that his fear and sorrow came from a new story he carried with him and could not tell. Not yet. He held it in his heart and waited, traveling always toward the foothills that marked the end of the lowlands and the last leg of his journey.

Ahead lay The Mountains Covered with Smoke. He breathed the name in his own tongue. *"Sha-cona-gee."* It gave him courage. His home, and his last hope for a way out of destruction, waited for him there in the mother town of his people. There the Keetoowah, the wisdom keepers, lived. The untold story he brought to them weighed on his heart, a burden heavier than the pack he carried. Bone weary, they trudged on, declining pleas to stay and recover from the hardship of the trail. He had no time for rest. The end of the journey drew nearer every day, and the urgency to reach Sha-cona-gee became stronger with every step.

The lowlands gave rise to gentle hills that grew steeper, until they climbed into the high and misty mountains. Like smoke from a thousand pipes, mist reached toward the peaks and clouded the valleys. He turned his face into the cool wind that blew through the trees and trudged on, impatient to reach the end of this long and hurried trek. Across the first mountain, then through the gap of the next, he made his way. Too impatient to stop for long, they rested at night under the moon, then rose before dawn to walk through yet another long day.

The trail became wider, well-trod by traders, warriors, travelers, supplicants, and seekers who traveled this way to the place where the sacred fire burned in the seven-sided lodge on the mound. A thick carpet of leaves silenced their steps. One day more and they could see over the ridge to the end of their journey. The nearness of the mother town gave him hope and spurred him on step after weary step.

Sensing the end of the trail, the three dogs lifted their noses to smell the air. The travois packed with bundles of the few trade goods sent from other towns, rattled on the trail as they picked up their pace.

Tsi-s-qua stood taller, the pack he carried heavy with the weight from the travois of the dog that limped beside him, too tired to tow it any longer.

Odors of cooking fires and curing hides reached them on the wind, the unmistakable scent of people who live the way human beings lived everywhere he traveled, close together in their little towns and villages, drawn to each other like a buffalo is drawn to the herd.

Only he lived alone. He, the boy, and their dogs.

A chestnut tree spread heavily laden branches over the trail, marking a remembered boundary and the last leg of his travels. Recollections of home created an urgency that goaded him to find a reserve of strength that took him over the last ridge and beyond. At the rise, he looked down into the valley and saw what he longed for. Thin wisps of smoke drifted high above the trees in the distance, rising from the peak of the seven-sided council house atop the mound where the sacred fire burned. Before sunset they would be in the town of healers, a place where the wise Keetoowah kept the ancient ways and offered comfort to troubled spirits. Home, at the foot of the hallowed mound in the bend of the river. There he could unburden his soul.

The Keetoowah would know what to do about the coming of the Turtle People.

Nothing in his knowledge or in the stories he gathered from all the tribes and nations could save his people from the strangers who spread death wherever they walked. Their only hope resided with the wisdom keepers in the sacred mother town. This hope brought him from a faraway seacoast, across deserts plains and mountains to seek their guidance. It brought him home to the place of his birth and the elders who entrusted him with the mysteries.

He adjusted his heavy pack, his broad back straight despite the load, and strode ahead. The end of his journey came into view. In the walled town in the bend of a river where the seven-sided council house sat atop a mound in the center of the town, they could rest.

He paused on a hill and told Tsi-s-qua, "See where the smoke drifts through the trees? It rises from the sacred fire that unites all the clans of our people."

The sight of it lifted his spirits. The Keetoowah could not change fate, but they could share his burden and perhaps find a way to lessen the desolation. The ancient prophecy that foretold this day said nothing of a way out. It predicted the end of everything that gave purpose to their life.

The boy knew the story. The fire burned day and night since the ancestors built the mound and lit the fire atop it. It might burn low at times, a few living coals holding the spirit in their potential to flame strong when fed by the fire keepers, but always burning. In the days of the New Fire, when winter faded into spring, the clans gathered in the mother town. With every fire in their home villages extinguished, they came to celebrate the return of life to the land, and to fill a pot with the sacred fire and rekindle their hearths. It connected them as one people around one flame.

Tsi-s-qua repeated the story of the fire as he took in his first look at the place of legend. Fatigue gave way to excitement as nearness to the end of the journey infused him with new strength. It gladdened Twisted Hair's heart to hear the reverence in the boy's voice and to watch him stride with confidence down the hill toward the town. He would be a worthy successor to take up the staff of the storyteller when it passed into his hands. Tsi-s-qua saw the Turtle People come from the sea, and the desolation they left in their wake. He endured the hardships of the long journey from the coast without complaint and still held on to hope for their people. The mother town was as much a myth to him as anything in the stories, but he followed the holy man, trusting in their destination.

Twisted Hair breathed deeply of the crisp cool mountain air and lifted his voice in a song of the wisdom keepers. It honored the ancestors, the old ones who lit the sacred flame in the mother town, the grandfathers and grandmothers whose spirits lingered around the lodges. The boy joined him in the song, his voice proud and strong.

Two young boys gathering firewood with their mothers heard them and sounded the cry, *"The Twisted Hair comes."*

Their mothers echoed the shout. Twisted Hair, the holy man, had come back to them. Most knew him only by the fame that followed him, but they joined in the rejoicing. He was one of their own, returning home for the first time in many years.

"Go, tell the Ghigham and the Uku," a man called to his son.

Excitement spread down the trail. Cries of welcome greeted them around every turn. The women dropped their bundles of firewood and ran to meet Twisted Hair and the boy. The tired dogs caught the excitement. Tsi-s-qua set them loose. Free from the travois, they trotted toward the town, answering the call of the barking dogs at the gate.

"The Twisted Hair is here," the boys shouted, drawing the travois behind them, racing down the trail. Their cries reached the walled town. A welcoming band spilled out of the gate and rushed to meet them. Young men relieved Twisted Hair and Tsi-s-qua of their packs. They knew better than to offer to carry the massive heavy staff. Only the holy man could bear the staff of the storyteller.

The palisade around the mother town stood three times as tall as the tallest man. Formed of sharpened tree trunks standing on end, it presented a formidable barrier to any threat. At the gate, the people stood aside to let Twisted Hair enter first. The narrow entrance allowed access to only one at a time. Sharp angles denied entry to large animals. Bears and panthers couldn't go through, and human enemies knew better than to try. The boy followed with the three dogs.

Twisted Hair's heart warmed with pride at the ingenuity of his people. Single file, they made their way through the angled corridor until it opened on the town. Sturdy lodges lined a wide path that led to the steep mound at the center of the town. Corn, beans, and squash grew in lush abundance in plots among the lodges. Vines climbed walls, spilling gourds and large crookneck squash among the leaves. The cooking fires gave off mouthwatering aromas and spoke of peace and abundance.

The Uku waited inside to welcome him home. The years they spent apart fell away in the elder's presence. Twisted Hair's mind went back to the boy he used to be before he went away with the old Storyteller.

Age grayed the Uku's long braid, but he stood strong and straight, his arms open to receive the traveler. As the peace chief of his people, the Uku's fame reached Twisted Hair all the way to the lands by the sea. Tales of his wisdom, and memories from childhood, inspired the spark of hope that brought Twisted Hair home.

The woman beside the Uku stood as tall as Twisted Hair. She was a young warrior when he went away. Charged with his care when his father died in battle and his mother failed to survive the birth of her only child, the war woman claimed her sister's son as her own and assured his safety. Her fame reached him on his travels, first for her prowess in battle, but in time her strength, courage and wisdom, made her worthy to become the Ghigham, the beloved woman of her people. As the last speaker in council, her voice was the final one heard when a judgment must be made.

Her warrior dignity failed at the sight of him. She blinked away rare tears and reached to embrace him. The knot in his belly loosened. He no longer tried to conceal his fear. The Ghigham's keen eyes saw, and all the joy faded from her face. She skillfully maneuvered him away from the crowd and with the Uku beside them, walked ahead.

She spoke softly so the people who followed couldn't hear. "What has brought you home, my son?"

"A new story must be told. It's an unwelcome tale, but one we must heed," he said.

He could say no more when the young people drew closer and surrounded Tsi-s-qua, curious, and a little awed that he traveled with the holy man. Wise beyond his years, the boy led them away.

The Uku turned and spoke to the people. "The Twisted Hair is home, and we rejoice that his travels have brought him back to his people."

Shouts of welcome rose then stilled at a sign from the Uku. He was the chief of the mother town in times of peace, and a Keetoowah of great renown, but he bore his authority with the humility of a holy man. One with power such as his did not need to show a proud face.

Twisted Hair lifted the great staff high in salute. He must not let them see his fear or know how weary the journey left him. They must see him as the holy man who walked the land through all the tribes and nations, gathering wisdom from their stories and bringing them home.

With the staff raised high, he watched them take in the image that lived in all the stories of Twisted Hair and all the storytellers who came before. The richness of his clothing, his strong body and handsome face, were part of his legend. Long hair, twisted into thick ropes and bound with beaded leather cords, hung almost to his waist. Only he could wear his hair in this manner. It set him apart and gave him his name, marking him as one who could walk in safety among all the people of the land. Even the sworn enemies of his tribe honored the Twisted Hair. He was the holy man from the mother town, the storyteller who kept the wisdom of the people of all the tribes and nation. In the stories of a people, their past, future, and the knowledge of the sacred ways that kept them strong, resided.

Every eye strained for a closer look at the great staff, marveling at the carved depictions of the totems of the seven clans of his people. Its story came down through the generations, as much a part of his legend as the strange way he wore his hair. He watched them as they memorized each detail, knowing they would describe it to their children and grandchildren, just as their elders described it to them. At its top, the owl with four faces looked in all directions, standing guard over the clans and their stories. Everywhere he raised it, it spoke of the wisdom residing in the mother town in the bend of a river in Sha-cona-gee.

When he lowered the staff, and walked away with the Ghigham and the Uku, the crowd followed at a respectful distance.

The Ghigham halted the procession at the door of a small lodge and called out.

In answer to her call, a slender hand drew aside the

covering of the door. A young woman stepped out into the evening shadows.

"He will lodge with you while he is with us," the Ghigham said.

The young woman stood silently before Twisted Hair, her eyes modestly lowered, and quietly welcomed him into her home. The men who carried his packs placed them beside her hearth.

The Ghigham said, "her husband went away four seasons ago. He is not likely to return"

Twisted Hair saw the sorrow in the woman's eyes. She still hoped her husband would come back to her.

"A woman cannot live on hope," the Ghigham said.

The sad eyed woman held aside her door and welcomed Twisted Hair inside.

Her hospitality pleased him, and her gentle smile warmed his heart. The weariness of his journey dropped away and the burden of the story he brought lightened when he rested by her fire.

The men who carried his packs lingered outside, talking about the weight of their burdens, speculating about the riches they contained. Perhaps they held red jasper from the coast or turquoise from the west. They talked of trade goods to offer in exchange.

"He will want healing herbs to take to the lowland towns, and rattles made from deer hooves." Their voices carried through the log walls to Twisted Hair's ears. He remembered better times when he entered a town with trade goods and stories, when the people celebrated and gave him gifts, when he brought stories and news from afar. Before the strangers came to end their world.

The young woman went to prepare his food. He waited alone in her lodge until the Uku came, accompanied by Tsi-s-qua.

"Come with me to the river," the Uku said. "Sorrow covers you like a blanket and there is no harmony in you,"

The elder took Twisted Hair and the boy to the banks of the river and lit a bundle of sage and cedar. Twisted Hair let the smoke spread its purifying fragrance from the souls of his feet to the beaded cord that secured his twisted hair atop his head. Beside him, the boy accepted the healing smoke, then together they walked into the cold clear water and immersed seven times beneath the cleansing stream and prayed the seven prayers. Peace came to Twisted Hair's spirit as the river washed away the residue of grief. Images that haunted his sleep, memories of brutality the strangers inflicted on the people by the sea, flowed away with the rapids.

He rose from the water and went to stand on the rocky shore, savoring the cool breeze on his body. How long had he been out of harmony? He had to think back to remember the last time his spirit felt at peace. The day he entered the first village the strangers destroyed, and saw the dead and maimed they left behind, all harmony departed from him. Now, with his spirit restored and balance returned, his thoughts turned toward hope.

With the exuberance of youth, the boy shook the water from his hair and gave a whoop that echoed off the hills.

The Uku stood back, watching.

"He has learned well," Twisted Hair said. "My work will be in good hands when I walk over."

"You have many years left to hold the wisdom of the people," the Uku said.

Twisted Hair said nothing, but recent dreams showed him images of the boy raising the great staff and walking away. Even wisdom keepers were not safe from the Turtle People.

With harmony restored to his spirit, he drew strength to face a future in which an enemy without pity spread through the world he knew.

Within the Stories of Our People,
Lies Our Strength

 Night fell. Firelight leapt into the darkness and the people assembled in the shadows cast by the flames. Twisted Hair sat with the Uku by the fire, rested, well fed, and in harmony with his own people in the town of his birth. The air of celebration caught him in its spell and he moved to the rhythm of the drums as they echoed the heartbeat of the earth. Singers lifted their voices in a call to the gathering. The final stragglers arrived and found their place. A few surrendered to the lure of the drums and danced, the women with their heads held high, looking neither left nor right but keeping their eyes straight ahead as they glided toward the center of the circle. Their dancing feet drew strength from the earth. The dance was a prayer for the people and for all the beings of the world.

Twisted Hair watched the sad eyed woman lead the dance and lent his prayer to hers as she reached the center and began the return through the spiral that brought the earth's abundance to her people.

The men whirled, leaping toward the sky, lifting hearts and celebrating the strength of their people. Little boys joined the dance, raising young voices in cries that matched their fathers'. Tsi-s-qua danced with them. He danced in the manner of the people beside the sea, honoring the memory of the dead with the dance.

When the final stragglers joined the gathering, drums and singers faded into silence. The little ones found their places, the smallest on blankets beside mothers and

17

grandmothers, bigger boys in groups near the fire. Elder men and women stayed close to Twisted Hair.

Tsi-s-qua left the dancers and sat beside the Uku. Only the warriors standing guard atop the wall were left outside the circle.

A hushed voice spoke. "He is come. Twisted Hair brings the stories of our people."

A spark of excitement whispered through the crowd.

The silence deepened as Twisted Hair rose to his feet. He began as they expected, with stories for the children. Their solemn black eyes shone in the firelight. Even the smallest was still and quiet. . . waiting.

"Long time ago" he began, his voice, reaching out to the little ones. "Earth was covered with water."

All but the youngest recognized the story with nothing more said than these words.

"Ahhh," the old ones sighed, and settled down in comfort on their blankets, to listen once again. Never would they grow tired of hearing how the beloved mountains and valleys of their home came to be.

"Galun-lati was crowded. No one could find a place to be alone and the houses all sat side by side. The trails and forests were filled with voices and there was no silence in the land, day or night. The people looked down at Earth and waited for the water that covered it to dry up. A long time passed, and water stood deep upon the Earth as far as they could see. They watched and hoped for a dry place to appear where some of the people of Galun-lati could live, but no land could be seen. Perhaps an island existed amid the water and they could not see it from so far away. They needed someone with the courage to go down to the world below and seek out that island.

A small grey dove, from a flock that filled the forest, gazed down upon the water and dreamed of a tree of her own in which to build her nest. She was not the strongest of the people of Galun-lati, but she was brave. 'I will go,' she said, and on her soft wings she soared off the walls of the above world and down to Earth below.

She flew the circle of the world, searching for a dry place to land. No dry land appeared, no trees grew, only water met her gaze as far as she could see. With wings, so weary she feared she might fall into the water, she struggled back to the above world. Exhausted, she whispered, 'There is no place for us on the earth, no island where we can live, only water.'

With the passing of time, Galun-lati became more crowded. The people looked down to the world below, searching for signs of land that offered a home for them on the earth.

Raven flew to the walls. 'I am bigger and can fly farther than Dove. I will go search for land.' He flew from Galun-lati and soared around the circle of the earth. Water covered all the world. On and on he searched and still no dry land appeared.

With his wings so spent, he feared he could no longer fly, Raven returned to Galun-lati.

The people of Galun-lati watched and waited for the waters of earth to recede. The above world became more crowded. Once again, they looked for someone strong enough to go to the world below and seek a place to live.

Grandfather Buzzard, the oldest of all the people of Galun-lati, flew to the wall and looked at the world far below. 'I will go,' he said, and lifted his great black wings.

The people feared for his safety and called him to come back home. It was not good for a beloved elder to go into danger. Their cries followed him as he glided away, down through the clouds, to soar above the earth."

Twisted Hair lifted his arms, sweeping his robe wide at his sides. The flickering firelight cast a shadow behind him. Like great black wings, the shadow fluttered, then disappeared when he folded his arms across his chest.

The children would remember this as the night they saw the grandfather of the buzzards.

Twisted Hair continued his story.

"The people watched from the walls of Galun-lati as Grandfather Buzzard circled the earth, searching for a dry place where they could live. When darkness fell, he flew on through the night, and into the next day.

When his great wings drooped with fatigue, they feared he would fall into the water. 'Come home, Grandfather,' they called.

But Grandfather Buzzard would not give up. He struggled on in his weary flight until his wings could not rise above the water's surface. They dipped deep into the muddy bottom time and again. Each time he faltered, he summoned the strength to draw his wings from the thick mud, shake them free, and labor on. When he brought his wings from the depths of the water, the thick mud that clung to his feathers fell away and left great mounds rising high above the waves. Through the night, he kept up his weary flight until the last of his strength deserted him. His wings folded for the last time.

Morning broke to find him sleeping, tired but safe on the peak of a lofty mountain, created from the mud his struggles drew from the bottom of the water.

The people of Galun-lati looked down and saw the valleys and mountains of Sha-cona-gee. Grandfather Buzzard awoke from his rest and circled high above the mountains that would become the home of the Ani-yun-Wiya."

The great black wings swooped upward once more, and then away as Twisted Hair lifted his arms, then folded them. He sat down on the blanket and took the pipe the Uku offered.

They sat in silence, considering the first story every child learned, of how their beloved homeland came to be.

Then came the gentle voice of an old woman, a grandchild on her lap. "And his grandchildren still circle over the land, just as Grandfather Buzzard did when he brought the mountains from the deep water. In this they honor his memory."

Other elders spoke to the little ones, telling how their ancestors made this their home thousands of years ago, and how they would always live here for as long as the Ani-yun-Wiya endured.

They lifted their eyes to the dark shape of the mountains that encircled their valley and whispered prayers of thanksgiving for the mother town, the river that flowed beside it and the mountains that protected it. The sacred mound rose at their back in the image of the mountains it honored. Ancestral spirits spoke in every breeze in the homeland of the Ani-yun-Wiya. With every breath, they breathed in the breath of honored ancestors.

A drum sounded a muted beat, and a lone singer raised his voice in a song to Sha-cona-gee, The Mountains Covered with Smoke. He sang of the hills and valleys they called home and the noble struggle of Grandfather Buzzard who raised them from the deep water.

In the expectant silence that followed, the storyteller listened while the Ani-Yun-Wiya considered the legend of the great buzzard.

The Uku spoke in his quiet way, "He did not have the beauty of the eagle or the sweet song of other birds, but he was one to be honored, for he too was part of the balance and harmony of all life."

Twisted Hair glanced at Tsi-s-qua, sitting in silent contemplation, listening to each story and song, attending every observation made by the people. He had learned to hold all these things in his heart against the day when he would be the storyteller. The store of knowledge gained in this way, was far greater than that known by many an old man.

Twisted Hair drew from the pipe and watched the spiral of smoke drift up toward the darkening sky. A young man added wood to the fire and laid a fresh cedar branch to smolder on the coals at the base of the flames. A cleansing, protective incense spread fragrance through the circle as it burned.

Twisted Hair passed the pipe to the Uku and stood. "It is not only Grandfather Buzzard who made Earth a good place for us. Other animal people give of themselves to make our lives pleasing. They have done so from the beginning."

The elders nodded in agreement as he continued.

"Long time ago when the first people were on Earth, the four leggeds, the water people, the feathered people, all looked at themselves and said, 'this is good.' They spoke of their rich thick fur, their shiny scales or soft feathers. They gave thanks to Unehlanuhe, the creator, for sharp horns or antlers, long claws or hooves. For their sharp teeth and for the way they could run fast or swim in the river or fly into the sky.

The animals grew strong and multiplied until there were many of them on the Earth. Their lives were good, but they looked at the poor two-legged people, the human beings and feared they would all die. The two leg-geds were naked. They had neither fur nor scales nor feathers. They had no horns nor antlers, no sharp hooves nor teeth or claws. They were not strong like Bear or fast like Rabbit. They were weak, cold, and hungry. Their children were too frail to survive through the bitter cold of winter. Many of them died and their numbers dropped until only a few remained.

In their wisdom, the animals knew all living beings were part of the sacred balance of life, and all the created beings were needed. If the human beings left the world, their place in the balance would be empty and all of life would suffer.

The animals came together in council and talked of ways the human beings might be saved.

Awi Usdi, the little white deer, chief of all the deer people, spoke to the animals. 'If the humans are to live they must have food that will make them strong, and shelter so their children can grow. We must give our-selves to the humans, so they can live.'

The animals agreed to sacrifice their own lives to save the humans, but they asked Creator to allow the spirits of the animals to return to Galun-lati when they died. If they willingly gave their lives to provide food for the humans, the humans must honor the animals and re-member the prayers and ceremonies that would send them to the above, world where they would remain until they returned, reborn in the forest.

The Creator of all things heard them, and it was so.

While the human beings slept, Awi Usdi walked among them and stirred their dreams. They dreamt of a little white dear who taught them the death song of his people and told them to sing it for the animals who of-fered their life as a sacrifice for the good of humans. The humans must honor the animals, taking only what they needed, and always sing the song that sent them to the above world.

When the humans awoke, they remembered the dream of a little white deer and the death song of his people.

From that day on, humans hunted the animals. They honored those who came to sacrifice themselves and sang the death song that sent their spirit home to the above world. With gratitude for the gifts of the animals, they took only what they needed. The human beings grew strong and their numbers increased. They were well fed, and the furs of the animals made warm robes that kept out the cold. Animal skins covered their lodges and kept them warm and dry even in the cold times. Children thrived and filled the villages.

For many generations, all was well with the humans. They lived in harmony with the animals and the balance of life remained.

As the generations passed, the humans forgot the dream of the little deer and the death song of his people. They celebrated the great hunters in the village and spoke of the pleasure they took in hunting. Many animals needlessly perished, and their bodies lay wasted in the forest. The hunters no longer honored the animals nor remembered the song that sent them to Galun-lati.

To make the kill easier, the humans formed a new weapon no animal could outrun. It reached out into the forest and brought the animals down. With his bow and arrow, a hunter could take many lives.

The animals feared the greedy humans might kill them all and destroy the balance they sacrificed themselves to secure. For the animals to survive, they must defend their kind from the hunters. They amassed to challenge the humans, but before they could get close, an arrow flew from a bow and an animal died.

To stand against the hunters, the animals must use the weapon they used. Bear made a fine bow, as good as the ones the humans had, but when he tried to shoot it, his long sharp claws became entangled in the bowstring and cut it in two.

Bear could not use the bow with his long claws. He bit them off and shot an arrow that reached its mark. He stood against the hunters and defended the animals until hunger made him weak. He tried to climb a tree to feed on the honey in a hive high in its branches, but without his claws, he could not. He tried to tear open an old tree trunk and feed on the grubs inside, but he needed his claws for that. Bear could not take off his claws to use the bow, Deer could not use it with hooves, raccoon had hands, but he was too small to draw back the bowstring.

Again, the animals called to Awi Usdi and told him how the hunters wasted the gift of the animals. The humans began to hunt because I came to them in a dream and offered our flesh and skins to save them,' Awi Usdi said. 'They dishonored our sacrifice and endangered the balance of life. Tonight, when they sleep, we will speak to them again.'

That night as the humans slept, Awi Usdi walked among them once more. He reproached the sleeping people for the way they dishonored the animals who gave their own bodies to save them. He reminded them of their promise to take only what they needed.

'You dishonored your promise and broke your word. You wasted the animals and forgot to offer prayers and songs to send them back to the above world. You left their bodies to decay in the forest and took lives you did not need to take. From this day on, if a hunter takes only enough to provide the needs of his family, and if he honors the animals who sacrifice their lives, you, will be strong. But the hunter who betrays the gift of the animal people, will suffer. Your body will wither and ache, and your hands will not hold a bow.'

When the human beings awoke in the morning, they remembered dreams of the little white deer who warned them of their selfish ways. Some of them felt ashamed for the way they dishonored the gift of the animals. They vowed to take only enough, and to always say the prayers that sent the animal home to the spirit world. Those hunters stayed strong and healthy and lived long lives.

Other hunters said, 'I too dreamed of the little white deer, but his warning means nothing to me.' They forgot his words and went on with their ways, wastefully killing the animals and failing to honor them as Awi Usdi told them to. For them it was as the little deer promised. They suffered. Their bones ached. Their joints became swollen and stiff. Their hands twisted and knotted into claws that could not hold a bow. In pain, they lived and died.

It is so to this day. The hunter who honors the animals and offers gratitude for their meat, taking only what is needed and leaving the rest to live, stays strong and healthy. The hunter, who does not, suffers."

A man near the fire pulled his blanket closer, hiding his gnarled fingers between its folds. He hung his head when young boys looked his way. Not long ago, he stood strong and straight, boasting of his skill as a great hunter and the pleasure he took in the kill. Now he could only hide his crooked hands that were unable hold a bow and remember how he always brought home more meat than his family could eat.

Twisted Hair saw the hunter's unease and the way the young men looked at him. He sat back on the blanket and let silence seal his words in their hearts. They would think of Awi Usdi and the other animals who lived in the stories. Within their thoughts, the lessons would linger and bring about respect and gratitude for the animal people.

From the edge of the crowd, a hunter's voice lifted in a song he always sang as he made his way through the thickets and forests. The song came down through generations of his family, given to his ancestor by a snake chief. It kept him and his descendants safe.

When the song ended, a voice came from the silence. "Tell us the story of Yellow Rattler's song."

A look of infinite sadness settled over the hunter's features as he told of the gift of a sacred song.

"Long time ago, when the animals still spoke with human beings, a war chief of our people left his family to go hunt. He knew his wife and sons were safe because there was peace with all the created beings after many generations of war. A hard law kept the peace, the law of retribution. The law said that any harm you did to another, could be avenged in like measure by his people.

The war chief's wife was hard at work grinding corn for bread while she watched her children. Her little one crawled into the grass and then began to cry. She ran to see what frightened him. There at his feet, coiled as if to strike, was a great red rattlesnake.

As is the way of a mother, all thoughts left her mind except the safety of her child. The grinding stone was in her hand. Her fear made her throw harder than she intended and instead of frightening away the snake, the heavy stone crushed his head.

Her regret could not restore Red Rattler's life. She sent her older son to take the dead snake to a place beside a trail his people used, so they would find him.

Her husband knew nothing of this as he traveled toward a valley where game was plentiful. As he neared the valley, he heard many mournful voices lifted in a death song. He listened, long enough to know they mourned the death of a great chief.

Climbing to the top of the ridge, he looked down to see a gathering of all the snake tribes, weeping around the body of Red Rattler. Their grief touched his heart. He went to them and asked, 'Who is so beloved that his death could cause such sorrow?'

Yellow Rattler, the war chief of the snakes answered him. 'Our great peace chief, Red Rattler was killed today in your town.'

The man wept, overcome by sorrow and remorse. He stayed with the snake people, grieving with them, making offerings and honoring Red Rattler. He sang the snake chief's death song with his people, and then sat outside their council house while Yellow Rattler and his warriors spoke of retribution for Red Rattler's death.

Yellow Rattler came to him and said. 'By the law of retribution, the death of our chief must be avenged. The council says that all who live in your town must die before your people and mine can live in peace again. Today, I will lead my warriors against your people.'

The man pleaded with the council. 'I am a war chief of my people, just as Red Rattler was your chief in times of peace. Take my life and your chief is avenged. Spare the life of the people in my town, for surely only one is guilty of slaying your chief.'

The council replied that he, of all his people, was most innocent. His death would do nothing to avenge Red Rattler. The warriors made ready to attack the town.

The man followed Yellow Rattler, beseeching him to spare his people. 'One in my village is guilty of this great wrong,' he said. 'If you will not accept my life as retribution for the life of Red Rattler, then take the life of his murderer and let the innocent ones in my town live.'

Yellow Rattler said, 'my brother. If we agree to do this, will you bring the murderer to me?'

With a heavy heart, the man agreed to do as Yellow Rattler asked. He would betray one in his town to spare the life of the rest. There was nothing more he could do.

In great sadness, the two warriors set out to the man's town, Yellow Rattler and the man. As they traveled, they talked of the burden of their duties and the need to keep the hard-won peace by observing the law of retribution.

In the town, they passed the lodges of the man's clan and others of his people. At each door, he thought of the ones who lived there, hoping it was not this one he must send to Yellow Rattler.

When the only lodge left was his own, grief made him falter. Yellow Rattler said, 'It must be done, my brother, or my people will come tomorrow, and no one will be spared.'

With grief so great he could not speak, the man could only nod in agreement.

'Send your wife to the spring for fresh water,' Yellow Rattler said. 'I will be there.'

The woman welcomed her husband and put food before him.

'I would like fresh cold water from the spring,' he said.

She took the water pot and went for fresh water. He sat with his children, waiting.

'Father,' his son said. 'I heard my mother cry out.'

'Be still, my son,' the man said.

They waited, and the woman did not come with the water. Instead, Yellow Rattler came to the house and coiled in the doorway. 'It is done,' he said. 'The price is paid. Your people are safe. My people grieve with you as you have grieved with us. Never again will you or your children's children need to fear the snake people. I give you a song. Sing it when you travel in our land and my people will honor it and leave you in safety.'

To this day, my clan sings Yellow Rattler's song. We live as brothers with his people."

The man softly sang the song that protected generations of his family from snakebite. When his song was done, he could hear the elders speaking to the children of the great price the man's ancestor paid to save his people and keep peace between the snakes and the human beings.

The stories, the songs, and the silence continued as a full moon climbed into the sky. Most of the stories, the people knew for they were of the kind told around the fire. Other legends were meant for a time when only the wisest elders listened. Twisted Hair kept those stories in his heart and waited. They were sacred, each word repeated in the same manner down through the generation to the worthy who preserved them. These stories held the mysteries and kept the people strong. If they were lost, the power that preserved the Ani-yun-Wiya died with them.

Twisted Hair told stories he acquired during his travels, stories told at firesides like this, by people far away. One was a strange story he learned from a wandering band on the plains. It told of the creation of the world, but in a different way. Their creator was a woman who wove all things into existence. She spun a web, and in the web, all the people, animals and the green growing things came into being. The all-powerful creator woman was unseen, and greater in size than the earth. In her natural state, she lived without form or substance. When she chose to take a shape, she appeared as a spider. The plains people who told her story called her Grandmother Spider.

Distant calls of the night birds echoed in the hills. The firelight flickered in the shadows like dancing ghosts in the darkness beyond the circle. Twisted Hair gave the people time to consider the strange new story he learned around the night fires of a faraway people. In time, the Uku raised his head and spoke. Everyone heeded his voice, for he was wise and his medicine strong.

"This is good for us to tell the children. Grandmother Spider has all power and can take any form she wishes, but she honors one who is among the smallest and most humble of all creatures when she takes the form of the spider. This we must remember. Even the smallest is worthy of honor for she is a part of the balance."

The Ghigham nodded. "Even with her great power she takes a humble form for herself. She knows the danger of too much pride."

Her words pleased Twisted Hair. He remembered a time when the Uku warned her about the danger of vanity, long ago, before he went away with the old storyteller. The acclaim she earned as a young war-woman made her prideful and vain. She did well to learn from Grandmother Spider's story.

The Uku spoke again. "Our people have not always remembered how the overbearing pride of a few can bring trouble to all. The way my grandfather told it to me was that long before our time, lived a family called the Ani'-Kut ani. They knew all the stories and had strong medicine. Their house stood atop a mound, just as our council house stands today. In those days, the mound where the house of the Ani-Kut-ani stood, was filled with the bones of their dead. They claimed to draw power from the dead bones. For a few generations, the Ani'-Kut ani cared for the people, keeping the raven mockers from the sick so they couldn't take their hearts and steal their last days of life, adding it to their own. Our people feared the Ani'-Kut ani, but their power kept us safe from sickness and harm.

As their power increased, so did their pride. They took what they wanted without regard for the needs of the people. They no longer cared for the weak or protected the sick. If they desired a woman they paid no heed that she had already taken a husband, or that she did not consent. They took her for their own without respect for her wishes. They claimed the right to do whatever they wanted because they were born Ani'-Kut ani. They said they were descended from the immortals and could speak with the spirits. Our ancestors lived in fear of them.

The time came when a young man with a good name went away to hunt. When he returned, his wife was gone, taken away by the Ani'-Kut ani. His grief and anger made him brave. The people had waited for one with the courage to lead them against the evil people. They followed the brave young man up the mound and slew all who were of the blood of the Ani'-Kut ani and added their bones to their ancestors in the mound.

Never, since that time, has any one family held a place of power over our people. Sacred knowledge is given only to those who are chosen by The Great One, and the creator of all does not care what family or clan they were born to."

A respectful silence held until the Uku took his seat and raised the pipe to his lips. They watched as he drew deeply one time, and then passed it on, his eyes on the thin curl of smoke drifting up into the darkness. He was a man whom The Great One had chosen. They trusted him with their sick and they knew the raven mockers feared him.

Twisted Hair thought about what he heard. The Uku's story brought to his memory towns he traveled through, built around earth mounds, ruled by chiefs who held power by virtue of their blood. Some he visited suffered under rulers as corrupt as the Ani'-Kut ani, but their people did nothing to protest. Here in the highlands, away from the weakness and decay he sensed in some of the lowland towns, lay strength. The people in this sacred town honored the ways of wisdom and healing. Any hope of prevailing against the coming of the Turtle People, resided here among the mountains. He did well to bring his story to the Keetoowah. They would know what to do. He looked at the Uku beside him. The people of the town must remember to always show due honor to the elders.

He took the pipe one more time, then stood. The ominous tone of his voice held a warning. "It is good you have a trusted holy man with the power to keep away evil. In a village, not far from here, the raven mockers took many an elder, and even young people who were wounded or sick. They were seen flying high among the clouds, their arms outstretched like wings with fiery sparks trailing behind them. Their beating wings made a sound like a strong wind, and in the wind, came the cry of the raven. All who hear that sound are afraid, for when the raven mocker cries in the night, we know a life will soon be taken.

Every town needs a strong Uku with medicine powerful enough to banish the skin changers. If a town is not protected, the raven mocker takes the form of a raven and flies unseen into a house. When no one is looking, he steals the heart of the sick one he finds there. He leaves no scar to betray the deed. The victim is left dead. When the raven mocker eats the stolen heart, he devours all the life it still holds and, in this way, prolongs his own days in the world.

Long ago when I was a boy traveling with the Twisted Hair before me, we lodged in a town where a young man went out hunting. The deer were scarce. When the evening shadows fell, and darkness drew near, he had made no kill and had nothing to show for a day of hunting. It shamed him to think of going home to his wife without meat for his family. He had already traveled far from home, but he trudged on toward the setting sun. Over the rise, he saw a house all by itself in the forest. Beside it stood a little asi. He had heard of this house. It was said that an old man and an old woman lived there alone. The hunter was glad to find a warm place to sleep for the night. He would rest awhile in the asi and hunt again in the morning.

When he reached the house the man and woman were not home. He called out to them, but no one answered. He went to the asi and stooped down to look inside. Just as in his village, the little sweat lodge was used for sleeping on cold nights. A small fire could keep it warm. Coals still smoldered in a fire in the center of the room, but he saw no sign of the man and woman. The hunter was bone tired and the asi felt warm. He crawled to the far side and curled up against the wall. Before he could fall asleep he heard the howl of a strong wind outside, and in the wind, the cry of a raven. The wind died as suddenly as it came, and the raven went silent.

A dark shadow fell across the door. The hunter shivered with fear. He huddled close to the wall of the asi and tried not to make a sound as he watched the man bend over and crawl inside. The man stirred the coals and added wood to the fire. Flames crackled and soon the smell of roasting meat filled the little round sweat house.

Careful not to betray his presence, the hunter raised himself and looked. The man held a stick over the fire. It speared through a heart that sizzled in the flames.

Again, a strong wind roared outside. The sharp cry of a raven came even louder than the wind. The shadow of a great black bird darkened the door. Then the wings folded, the shadow shriveled, and an old woman stood in the doorway. She crawled into the asi and sat across from the man.

The hunter's courage failed him. He trembled with fear when he heard what the man and woman said.

'How many did you get?' the woman asked.

'Only one,' the man answered, 'and I need it all. How many did you get?'

The woman hesitated. When the man asked again, she said, 'I went to a town to take the heart of a warrior who was hurt. The Uku there was too powerful for me. His medicine turned me away and would not let me enter the town. I am hungry. And I'm beginning to feel very old.'

Now, the hunter knew for sure he was in the asi of raven mockers, the most feared of all the skin changers. And to make matters even more frightening, one of them was hungry. He could hear his heart beat faster and louder.

The woman must have heard him. She took a flaming stick from the fire and swept it through the air, shinning its light to every recess of the asi. The hunter held his breath and hoped she wouldn't see him, but the light found him.

The woman dropped her torch and lunged for him. The hunter leapt aside and fled out the door, running faster than he had ever run before in all his life. He reached the cover of the trees when he heard the woman's hungry raven call. Her wings sounded like a rushing wind as she took to the air. Keeping to the shelter of the forest, he ran. The raven mocker flew above. . . hunting."

Twisted Hair paused and reached for the pipe. The moon drifted behind a cloud. The firelight within the little circle made the world beyond its flames seem darker. Not a word was spoken while everyone thought of the dreadful danger the hunter faced. Alone, in the dark woods with a hungry raven mocker stalking him from above.

Twisted Hair gave the pipe to the Uku and continued. "He escaped by running through a grove of cedar where evil could not follow. It was almost morning when he came home and told us of the raven mockers.

His people knew about the house that stood alone in the forest, and that a man and woman lived there. But they didn't know the man and woman were skin changers. Now, they understood why so many elders died in their sleep when they were still strong and healthy.

The hunter asked us to go with him to the home of the raven mockers. It is said they hunt at night and sleep while the sun is up. We followed him to the house in the woods.

Late that evening we reached the house in time to watch the sun set over the western mountains. As twilight fell, we knew we must hurry.

The hunter went to the door and called out, 'Grandmother. Grandfather. Are you here?'

No one answered.

He opened the door and we looked inside. We saw them lying on blankets spread on the floor, sound asleep. We were not afraid of them while it was still light outside. They only had power to harm us in the dark.

The last rays of the setting sun lit the sky, giving us a few more moments of safety, until darkness fell, and they awoke.

The women gathered cedar branches and placed them around the house. It is known that evil beings like raven mockers cannot cross cedar. This would keep us safe after nightfall.

We didn't know what else we could do then. I was but a young boy who knew nothing of such things. They asked the Twisted Hair, but he did not know how to slay skin changers. The wise elders believed there was no way to kill them, because they would become ravens and fly away. The warriors were willing to go against them, but their arrows and spears had no power against supernatural beings. We were all afraid, for many in the town had died before their time. We talked of how the raven mockers took them, stealing the last days of their life.

While we stayed beyond the circle of cedar and wondered what to do, flames rose from the cedar branches. The old holy man, who knew all the ways of the evil ones, held a crystal in the last rays of the setting sun and aimed its beam at the branches until they caught fire. The fire spread fast and soon the flames engulfed the house. Fed by the rich sap of the cedar branches, the fire consumed the old house and soon left nothing of the house but cinders and ashes where it stood.

I watched with the old Twisted Hair as the warriors prodded among the ashes and gathered up a pile of blackened bones. That's all we ever found of the skin changers. The raven mockers, who preyed upon the elders, the sick, and wounded of the town died in the fire set by the holy man and his crystal."

Around the fire, the people expressed their approval. It was good that the holy man knew how to kill the raven mockers. No one was safe when skin changers hunted among the lodges, preying on the sick and old.

Twisted Hair raised his eyes to the darkened sky and stood still and quiet, listening to the people talk of how they no longer had to fear the skin changers. Raven mockers had not troubled them for as long as anyone could remember. They only lived in the stories of long ago.

Twisted Hair said nothing. He just watched the sky. The people fell silent when they took note that he seemed to be searching for danger, as if he thought some threat might come sweeping down from the night.

When silence settled over the circle, a silence so deep his softest voice could be heard by all, he said, "They say the man and woman had children."

A shudder ran through the crowd as they too looked at the sky. Some murmured about how fortunate they were to have an Uku with medicine so strong he could keep skin changers away, and young men and women who learned from him. Others talked of how people came from many tribes to listen to the wisdom of the Uku, the Ghigham, and the other holy people who kept their village strong.

Many promised to bring gifts to the old holy man. "I'll bring a bearskin robe to keep him warm this winter," a hunter said.

Twisted Hair gave a slight nod to the Uku. He would have plenty of tobacco, meat, corn, and anything else he needed before tomorrow ended, but the night was still young and there were other stories to tell.

A young warrior told of how his grandfather once saw Uktena, the great serpent.

"Tell the story your grandfather told you," Twisted Hair said.

The young warrior repeated the story he learned at his grandfather's knee. "The great serpent coiled around a mountain with his monstrous head resting on the peak. The crystal 'Ulunsu-ti' crowned his head and glowed blood red in the sun. Many brave warriors went against Uktena, seeking to slay the serpent and claim the Ulunsu-ti for there is no greater power than the Ulunsu-ti. Only the one who kills the serpent can take the talisman from his head. Many craved the power it could give them and died trying to take it. An outsider came and used his sorcery to kill Uktena. He took the Ulunsu-ti and uses it till this day. We have nothing to fear from that worm. He will never be a threat to us again."

The Uku rose to his feet. He had the attention of all his people for he held the knowledge and power that healed their sickness and kept away harm. "Do not speak lightly of Uktena or the Ulunsu-ti." His voice held a warning. "There was a time when the serpent took many lives of the Ani-yun-Wiya. When his life begins, he is no bigger than a grub. He can only eat small things when he is young. No one is afraid of him then, for he is seldom seen. But he grows fast. And as long as he lives, he grows. First, he eats mice, then rabbits. Soon he is of a size that such small animals are not enough to satisfy his hunger. He hunts for bigger game. Man, or animal, it matters not to Uktena. When he has eaten everyone and everything, he moves on and finds more. No one is safe when Uktena is in this world.

I do not doubt that this man's grandfather saw him. The serpent lived near here, on the mountain where nothing grows. His blood and poison are what made the mountain bare.

In another town, there lived a proud warrior, a con-juror who boasted of his strong medicine and his might in battle. Men who lost many of their people to Uktena, heard him boast. If he was so strong, perhaps the foolish braggart could use his might against Uktena. The men captured him and refused to release him until he agreed to find and kill the serpent. Tempted by the power the Ulunsu-ti could bestow, he agreed.

The warrior traveled the land, seeking the place where Uktena lay in hiding, for he was foolish enough to think the serpent was small enough to hide or had need to. In one town, the people led him to a cave and told him the serpent was there. He killed the monster inside, but when he went to claim the Ulunsu-ti from its head, he found only a great toad lying dead in the cave. When he came to the mountain where Uktena lived, he saw the monstrous serpent's body coiled around the mountain all the way to the top. Only when he looked at the size of the monster's head and sharp fangs, did he become humble enough to call upon Creator for help.

"Unehlanuhe heard his call and showed him the only way the life of Uktena could be taken. The foolish man listened and did as he was told. It was not through his own knowledge that he killed the serpent but with the wisdom of the Great One.

He was too ashamed of his boastful ways to return to his own people who knew him as a proud and arrogant conjuror. When he claimed the Ulunsu-ti from Uktena's head, he made an oath to use it and the power it gave him for the good of the people who took him to live among them. He keeps his vow, but he grows old and soon will walk over to the above world. The man who holds the Ulunsu-ti after him must be strong."

The Uku sat down and drew on the pipe.

The warrior spoke again. "The Uktena is dead and we no longer need fear him."

The Uku said, "Uktena cannot die. He is a being who lives forever. He waits within the Ulunsu-ti until he is freed to take form, then once again he will grow until he is as fearsome as the great serpent he was before. Someday another will need to kill him before he eats everyone. There will be many who try. Greed for the Ulunsu-ti will make them brave, but it will take more than greed and courage to slay the Uktena."

For a while the people talked about the danger of Uktena and the many stories they heard of him. Some claimed he had been seen again.

The Uku listened with lowered eyes. Twisted Hair watched him and knew why he looked troubled. He had seen the bundle secreted away in the holy man's lodge, well-guarded by a trusted warrior. The Uku's sleep would be forever haunted by the monster and the battle he fought, but he used the crystal well for all the years since he claimed it from Uktena. His people were safe and good things came to the village. Yes, when rightly used, the Ulunsu-ti could be good medicine. With the help of the Nunne'hi, the Uktena would remain imprisoned inside the crystal where he could do no harm.

The once proud and boastful conjuror was now the wise and humble Uku who served his adopted people well.

Another told of seeing the Dakwa swimming under his canoe, and said he feared the great fish would devour him as it had so many others. Some told of the times when human beings and animals could speak to each other. Great warriors and hunters were remembered, and their deeds recalled.

An old woman told of a boy she knew when she herself was just a child. "Many times, I helped his sister look for him when he wandered away. His sister scolded him and told him to stay with the other boys, but he would forget. One day he walked away, and we could not find him.

When he came home he looked no different than when he left. The clothes he wore were the same. Nothing about him had changed, but his sister and I were different. Since he was lost, we grew old enough to have children and grandchildren.

The boy cried for his mother, but she had long since walked over to the above world. The people who were children with him, were now old, and he was still a boy. When we asked him where he had been for so long, he said he had only been gone three days. He followed the music he said, and the sound of dancing, until he found where it was coming from. He hid for a time and watched the dancers. They were little, no taller than his knee and beautiful to look at. They found him when the grass he hid in tickled his nose and made him sneeze. He was afraid, but they were kind and took him to their village. There he stayed and was well fed and cared for until they sent him home.

He took us to the place where they lived. He said their village was very beautiful with ripe corn fields and great chestnut trees. We found nothing in that place but a hedge of laurel around a bare hillside.

The boy cried for a long time. He cried for his mother, father, uncles, aunts and grandparents, and for all his friends who became men and women, not the children they were when he went away. All the elders were gone, the young people grown old. In the land of the little people, the Yunwi Tsunsdi, time passed slowly. Only three days went by for the boy in their world, but many years came and went in the town of his people."

The woman said no more, just sat still and watched while the children thought about her story. It served its purpose. The little ones would remember it and be careful of wandering far from home. They didn't want to be taken away by little people, to come home and find everything changed, their parents old or dead and their friends all grown up while they remained children. The mothers smiled at each other over the heads of their little ones.

Someone asked a mother to tell about the Nunne'hi woman who helped her find her lost child who roamed too far from home. The people smiled, for no one feared the immortal Nunne'hi. "Was she beautiful, and strong?" they asked.

"All Nunne'hi are strong and beautiful," she answered. "It is good they live inside the mountain overlooking our town. We will always be safe with the immortals so close to our home."

An old man repeated an oft-told tale of the time the Nunne'hi took him to their town and cared for him after an injury. "I would not be alive today if not for the immortals," he said. "When I fell through the ice and could not move, a Nunne'hi man found me and carried me through the stone face of the mountainside and into his town. A river clear as the air ran past fruit trees bearing fruit and blossoms. The scent of ripe peaches filled the air. In the corn fields, green corn and roasting ears both grew on the same stalk. Never have I seen a more beautiful town or kinder people.

I rested in a fine lodge on soft robes until my wounds healed. When time came to go home, they took me beyond a grove of blossoming apple trees with ripe fruit hanging thick on the branches and pointed me to the right path. Don't look back, they said, but when I stepped beyond the grove of trees and into the snow, I longed to see the sunshine again. I looked back and saw nothing there but the bare stone of the mountain side, as smooth and without feature as it is to this day. No doorway remained, and nothing marked the entrance to their world. I stood alone in the cold and knew I could not return."

"It is always that way with the Nunne'hi," the Ghigham said. "They and their lands cannot be seen unless they wish it. Only a few are allowed inside. When they leave, they can never find the way back, though they always try. Once you see their world, it always calls to you."

Late into the night the stories continued. Some of the children fell asleep and mothers carried them inside. The boy stayed at the storyteller's side long after the rest of the young ones left the fireside. He spoke not a word but listened to everything.

At last, only the Uku, the Ghigham and the wisest Keetoowah remained by the dying fire with Twisted Hair and the boy. Now, the story that weighed down his spirit and troubled his dreams must be told. The moonlight cast a shadow on worried faces, waiting to hear what he held back until this moment. He spoke quickly, to tell a story that would change everything for the wisdom keepers and all their people.

"A new evil has come to our land. He wears a white skin and looks at the world through pale eyes. Where he walks, death comes with him. His weapons kill with the sound of thunder. When he goes away he leaves behind the bodies of our dead and a sickness that takes many that escape the slaughter. They say these evil men came from the sea bringing desolation from their faraway land."

"Have you seen this enemy?" The Ghigham asked.

"We saw them, Tsi-s-qua and I," Twisted Hair said. "First, in a town by the sea. When we realized, they fulfilled the prophecy of the Turtle People, we hurried here with the story. Not far away from the coast, we came near a large and prosperous town with many strong warriors. We heard loud voices speaking in a strange tongue, and anguished cries from the people of the town. Smoke and flames rose from the lodges. The strangers took what they wanted and set fire to the rest, leaving dead and wounded alike to be consumed by the flames. We saw them ride away, glinting like mica in the sun. They dragged bound captives behind them.

I came to that town many times before and saw strong people reaping a rich harvest. On that day, only a few still lived, weeping over the dead. An old man said the evil men killed without mercy, hacking them to death with their long knives. Most of the warriors lay dead with the rest, unable to defeat an enemy clothed from head to foot in shining shells that protected them from arrows."

"The prophecy is fulfilled. The Turtle People have come," the Ghigham whispered. "Visions foretold a time

45

when men with shells like turtles would come from the sea and bring with them the end of the world.

"They are here," Twisted Hair said. "We went to a city by the sea where they were first seen and saw suffering beyond anything we have ever known. I hurried back to Sha-cona-gee, hoping the Keetoowah could find a way to save us. If there is no hope and all is lost, I would die here with my own people."

The Uku's voice trembled. "We knew this day would come. Since the ancestors first foretold it, we searched our knowledge for a way to turn it aside. There is nothing we can do."

Twisted Hair gave them the only morsel of comfort he had. "It is a long way from their ships to the mother town of our people here in Sha-cona-gee, and many strong warriors defend all the trails and river passages. For now, we are safe here in the mountains covered with smoke."

The rising sun found the elders still sitting by the smoldering embers with Twisted Hair and Tsi-s-qua. Their wisdom held no answers. Even the Uku possessed no medicine to turn aside an evil such as this.

Dawn found them on the banks of the river. Hopelessness robbed them of harmony and they looked to the healing water to restore them. Seven times under, each time with an urgent prayer to the Above Beings for protection and guidance. They emerged with purity of purpose, in harmony with Spirit and with their people, but with no more hope for survival than before.

"There is purpose in all things," the Uku said.

The days continued without change. Twisted Hair and Tsi-s-qua fell into the pattern of life in the mother town. Tsi-s-qua thrived, living as the other boys lived, learning the ways of the young in the mother town. He hunted, fished, and became skilled in the games they played. But when the elders gathered in the council house around the sacred fire, he was always there. When stories were told, and the elders talked, he listened. When he spoke, his words were wise.

At first, they kept the arrival of the Turtle People from all but the small group of elders. It served no purpose to tell them of the strangers beyond the mountains when there was nothing they could do. The walls around the town held strong and warriors stood ready to defend it. Meat and fish dried on racks against the cold times when it might be scarce. Gardens promised a rich harvest and abundant stores. The mother town could withstand danger from man or nature, but the Turtle People brought a new threat.

Days and nights passed in the healing village. The knot of fear that tormented Twisted Hair eased its grip while he rested in the lodge of the gentle woman. It pleased him to see that sadness no longer clouded her eyes and she smiled when he sat at her fire.

For the first time since he left the war woman's house to travel with the old storyteller, he felt at home. He grew up on the trail, knowing any comfort he found would soon end. The only constant was the old storyteller and the journey, until the old storyteller died in his sleep, far from friendly firesides or warm lodges. Alone, and too young for the duty that fell to him, he dug a grave and laid his only companion to rest. Beside the grave, he twisted his hair for the first time, took up the staff, and set out alone. Memories of those long days and nights of lonely hardship faded. Contentment was a new emotion, and he savored it, knowing it couldn't last.

He dreaded the time when he had to leave the woman and the home they shared, yet he knew he must soon go.

His work called him to the lands beyond the mother town where they waited for the storyteller to bring the stories of the people. He searched his memory for a legend that hinted at a way to save them from the Turtle People, but every story promised devastation.

Each day he sat in the council house with the Uku, the Ghigham, and the war chief, forming a plan to defend the mother town. The war chief sent his warriors to scout the trails for evidence that the strangers approached. Scouts traveled far to seek information and brought back nothing but rumors of strange men in distant lands. Warriors set a watch along the boundaries of their lands, challenging any who came nigh.

A morning came when the Uku and the Ghigham entered the young woman's lodge. The council had spoken, and Twisted Hair must go to the towns beyond the mountains and recount the story of the Turtle People.

"Tell them to send out scouts to look for signs of the Turtle People," The Uku said. "Learn all you can from them, and at the time of harvest, return and bring word to the mother town."

The young woman's smile faded and sadness once more darkened her eyes. "His place is here," she said to the Ghigham. "He is a holy man and keeper of knowledge and of our sacred ways. Twisted Hair is Keetoowah."

The Ghigham agreed. "The Twisted Hair is a holy man, but his work is beyond these walls and among our people wherever he finds them. Generations yet unborn will look to him for the knowledge cloaked in his stories. In the days of the children's children, they will still seek him. His wisdom will be needed even more in times to come." She spoke with her head held high, but sorrow echoed in her words.

The Uku embraced Twisted Hair. "Your road will be long, my son, and you will find no rest in this life." Infinite sorrow aged his features as if he gazed beyond the distant hills and saw the future of his people. "You must be strong and give what hope you can, even when there is no hope."

The Ghigham turned away quickly and hid her face. "We will leave you to prepare for your journey," she said, and hurried away.

Twisted Hair held the woman close while she wept, dreading the moment when they must part. She touched his face and pleaded with him to come back to her.

"I will return at harvest time," he said.

Her face mirrored his dread that their parting would be forever.

With the first light of dawn, he stole away from the lodge while the woman still slept. The boy waited for him at the gate. With the three dogs, they walked away from the only place in the land they called home.

Voices in the Wind

 Families harvested fish from their traps in the shallows, watching the tree line for movement. No children frolicked on the riverbanks now. They stayed within the walls and played at fighting enemies or making weapons. Somber women gathered firewood in the forest under the watchful eyes of warriors. Men chopped tall pines with stone axes and brought them to reinforce the walls, shoring up their defenses against the strangers.

Before the threat of the turtle people, the Keetoowah welcomed all who traveled through the mountains to the mother town. Now warriors kept watch on all the trails, granting passage only to those who proved their loyalty to the people. The war chief prepared for battle and sent out patrols to cover the boundaries of the land, ever vigilant against enemies.

The store of arrows and spears increased, with every skilled hand hard at work knapping flint and preparing shafts. Every child who was old enough to help trimmed feathers to affix to arrows. All the young men and many of the women followed the war chief to the forest where they honed their battle skills.

The people who lived in a town of peace, prepared for war.

The high heat of summer turned toward cooler nights and crops ripened in the fields. The village in the shadow of the mountains covered with smoke, remained quiet and secure. Visitors from many tribes and towns came to learn from the Keetoowah. Like past generations they traveled to the mother town seeking answers from the wisdom keepers. They brought with them rumors of strangers who killed, maimed, and took captives.

They all asked the same questions. "Are the strangers the Turtle People from the sea? What can we do to turn aside the end of our world?"

The Ghigham and the wisdom keepers told them the story of the seer who saw the vision of the Turtle People and his warning of an enemy who would come from the sea. First, he walked on six legs, then two. Shining turtle shells covered him from head to foot, turning aside the warriors' arrows. When this enemy came, he brought the end of the world.

"What is the meaning of the six legs, then two?" The visitors knew the story, but this was beyond their understanding.

"The seer gave us nothing to explain this strange saying," the Uku said. "Twisted Hair saw the strangers and helped us understand. They ride beasts with four legs, and when they alight, they walk on two legs, upright as men. Their shining shells are called armor. They wear it to protect them from arrows and spears. Word has come that they are vulnerable when they take it off. Some of our warriors have waited in ambush and fallen upon them while they slept. We have known a few victories in this way, but the enemy comes in greater numbers. Only a few at first, but more follow."

The visitors returned to their homes to tell their people what they learned in the mother town and warned them to prepare for the worst.

The woman who waited for Twisted Hair walked the trail to the top of the hill and watched for him until the Ghigham came for her and brought her home. They sat together beside her lonely hearth, sharing their fear that the man they both loved might never return to the mother town. The feel of peril reached out from the lands beyond the mountains.

The people kept the festivals and observed the cycles of seasons just as their ancestors did in generations past. Hunters brought food from the hills, the grain hung heavy on the stalks, chestnuts dropped from trees in abundance. The first hint of autumn tinged the leaves with the beginning of fall color, and no sign of the strangers appeared.

Warriors returned from patrol and reported that all was well.

Fear of the strangers diminished, and contentment returned to the mother town. Perhaps the encircling mountains protected them, and the threat would stay in the lowlands. The Ghigham listened and let them believe. It might be their last summer of peace. She hoped the memory might give them strength to endure.

Now, only the war chief and his warriors continued the watch for the strangers. The height of harvest season, preparing stores of food against the approach of winter, and getting ready for the celebration of earth's abundance kept the people of the mother town occupied. There was little time to talk of the Turtle People.

The Ghigham, the Uku, and the wisest of the elders did not forget. Foreboding of what the strangers would bring haunted them day and night.

"In their hands, they hold the end of the world," the Uku said.

The Ghigham nodded and said, "Yes, the end of our world."

***

On a day when corn ripened in the husk and the late summer sun warmed the land, the Ghigham gathered squash and beans among the tall cornstalks. With her basket full, she paused and turned her face to the soft breeze that came down from the mountain. It felt cool on her skin. She put down her basket and relished the wind blowing through her hair.

A voice, so soft she thought she imagined it, whispered in her ear. She stood still and listened. The whisper grew loud, insistent, speaking dire words that filled her heart with fear. She cried out in alarm, but the voice would not be silenced. She listened, while it told her of a fate that approached from the sea, and what she must do to save her people.

When the wind died down and the voice fell silent, she left her harvest basket among the cornstalks and ran. Women working with her in the field called to her,

but she rushed past them without answering. She hurried up to mound, into the council house, and found the Uku there, waiting. One look at his face and she knew. He too heard the voice in the wind.

"The Nunne'hi have spoken," she said. "It is as Twisted Hair warned us. The strangers will come. Our sacred ways, our songs and stories, all that keeps the people of the one fire strong and in harmony, will be lost. They say everything will change. They warn that countless numbers of our people will die and many who live will become like the strangers and forget our ways."

The Uku finished the message of the Nunne'hi. "Our people will be driven away, far from the sacred lands of Sha-cona-gee. The mother town will be abandoned and lost, the sacred fire extinguished. But they ask us to be sealed inside this mountain. To no longer be mortal but live as the invisible Nunne'hi. Is it the right thing?"

54

Tears spilled unheeded from the old man's eyes. The Ghigham sat beside him looking down at the town that stretched out to the bend in the river, spreading beyond to the shelter of the mountains, as it had through generations long passed from memory. It looked permanent, like part of the land that would last as long the mountains stood. The laughter of children, songs of women harvesting in the fields, and cries of warriors in mock battle drifted up the mound to their ears. How often had they listened without hearing the sounds of the mother town that would soon be silenced?

"The Ani'yun Wiya have received all people here to learn the sacred ways that keep us strong," the Ghigham said. "The Keetoowah welcome seekers who come to learn the wisdom of the ancestors. The sacred fire still burns as it has since the beginning, bringing harmony and unity to all who seek it. If this is lost, there is no hope for us. Our town, the wisdom keepers who live here, and the sacred knowledge we hold for the world, will all be lost if the strangers find us. The Nunne'hi say it will all be destroyed and our stories forgotten. They offer us a way to save it."

"Then, we must do as they ask," the Uku said.

The Ghigham sat in quiet thought. It was not the way of the Ani'yun Wiya to make decisions without listening to the people. To do as the Nunne'hi asked would affect everyone. "We will wait," she said. "Say nothing of this until we see if others hear the voices. Then we will take it before the council. This is a decision that must be made by all the people."

The Ghigham left the Uku and returned to her work, saying nothing of the voices to the contented women reaping a bountiful harvest.

Were she and the Uku the only ones who heard the

Nunne'hi speaking in the wind?

Evening came. In the lengthening shadows a hunter returned from the forest with his kill across his shoulder. The Ghigham felt the wind blow across her face. The voices whispered soft within it. The hunter's wife came to meet him. They both stopped and faced into the wind to listen. The Ghigham saw fear and confusion steal across their countenance.

She went to them. "Did you hear the voices?"

"Yes, Grandmother," they answered. "Is it true? Must we do as they ask?"

"Come with me to the council house. We must speak with the Uku," she said.

They found the Uku in the council house with the war chief and the council of elders. A fire keeper fed the flame and the sacred fire leapt high and burned red.

"We heard voices in the wind," the hunter said.

Through the open door, they watched the people of the mother town climbing up the mound. "Voices spoke in the wind," they said, as they took their places around the fire. Warriors, mothers, fathers, young, and old, soon sat in silence, waiting until all the people gathered. They waited for answers from the Uku, the Ghigham, and the elders.

The Uku spoke. "The Nunne'hi whispered in the wind, and we have heard what they want us to do. We are the keepers of the wisdom and the sacred ways of our people. They offer a way to preserve our knowledge for generations yet to come. Will you do what they ask of us?"

The war chief spoke. "Our lives here are long and contented. We are safe in this town of healers. Uneh-lanuhe has smiled on us. All the people who come here to seek wisdom and find harmony need our teachers. Sacred ways that have been forgotten in other villages are remembered here. For the sake of all the people, now and in generations to come, we must not go into the mountain. Our town is necessary to the world of mortals. They can't find us if we hide away with the Nunne'hi."

"Yes," the Uku said. "We are needed. That's why the voices speak to us. If we do as the Nunne'hi ask, we can stay as we are forever. We can keep the wisdom and ways of our people. When the rest who stay outside forget, we will remember. This is what the Nunne'hi ask us to do."

The war chief's duty to protect his people weighed heavy on him. "The immortals ask us to hide inside their mountain, never to see our world again. I cannot live here in safety while our people beyond this town face the enemy without us. Cowering in the land of the Nunne'hi is not the way of the Keetoowah warrior. We will face the strangers with the courage of a great people, not as frightened children gone to ground while others perish."

One by one his warriors rose to their feet to stand with the war chief. A warrior called out, "We do not fear the strangers. When they come, they will die. It is always so when an enemy comes against us."

A war cry rose from their ranks, echoing among the warriors outside as they took sides with the war chief.

The Ghigham lifted her hand for silence. "The voices that speak in the wind gave us seven days to make our choice. They first spoke yesterday, then again today. Two days are gone. Five are left." She turned to the war chief. "Send your warriors through the village to gather all the people who did not hear the voices, and bring them in. When all have spoken, we will decide."

The war chief obeyed the Ghigham. With a nod that showed his respect, he turned to give orders to his warriors. They set off to gather everyone to sit in council.

They came, their unease evident. One woman said, "I heard the voices in the wind, but I don't want to do what they ask of us. My sons have taken wives in towns beyond the mountains. Am I to go and leave them behind at the mercy of the strangers?"

Other voices spoke up, voicing concern for those left behind. A young man, his wife beside him and their infant between them said, "My mother and father, all my family live in another town. I will never see them again if we do what the Nunne'hi want us to do. Our son will never know them."

The Uku told them what he heard in the wind. "We are the keepers of knowledge unknown in the world beyond these mountains. Great devastation is coming to our people, and nothing can turn it aside. The Nunne'hi offer a way to save it until it can be restored to our children's children, perhaps many generations from this day. It is our duty to go to the land of the immortals where the knowledge we hold can be protected."

The Ghigham spoke of the danger they faced from the strangers. "They come from a strange land far away, and spread across our world, bringing destruction everywhere they walk. They will come to us, and our town will fall as have others before us. Everything we know, all the ways of healing and harmony, the stories that preserve the mysteries, memories of the ancestors, all will be forgotten. The Nunne'hi offer sanctuary within the mountain, but if we go with them, we can never return. These mountains and all our lands will be lost to us. Their world will be our only home."

Mothers held their little ones and worried about the peril the strangers brought to them. The Immortals offered safety for the children within the mountain. To refuse the offer of the Nunne'hi left the children at the mercy of an enemy who had no pity on young or old.

An old woman said, "You speak of safety, but we must also speak of loss. Our beloved homeland where the very earth is the bones of our ancestors and the wind is the breath they breathed, will be denied us. The world of the Nunne'hi lies far beyond this valley, the trails, the forests, and rivers. As much as I fear the strangers, I love Sha-cona-gee more."

Others agreed with her. "This is the homeland of our people. Refuse the Nunne'hi and tell them we choose to stay in our world and take our chances with the strangers. We have strong warriors to protect us."

The Ghigham listened in silence to everything they said, then spoke up. "Our purpose is to hold wisdom for our people. That is the reason the ancestors came to this town and why we are here. If we die, we take all we know with us. If we do as the Nunne'hi ask, our wisdom will be preserved. If we are alive, there is hope that we can bring it back for our children's children when our world is safe again. I will do as the Nunne'hi ask and en-ter the council house on the seventh day. I will wait for them to seal our town against the world and hope for a time when we can return."

In silence, they considered her words. A voice heavy with sorrow spoke, "Could it be that we must leave our homeland forever to fulfill our purpose for being here?"

The days passed, and they talked, each one giving voice to hope and despair. On the morning of the sev-enth day, only one young woman remained outside the council house. She faced the path through the pines and watched, yearning to see the Twisted Hair appear. It wasn't time for him to return, but she hoped against hope that the Nunne'hi called him home.

The Ghigham went to her side. "I grieve with you,

but he has work he must do."

In silent sorrow, the young woman dried her tears and went inside to wait with the rest for the Ghigham to speak.

All the people of the village crowded into the council house, some still questioning the decision to obey the Nunne'hi.

The Ghigham lifted her hand and a hush fell on the people. She was the last speaker, her words the final ones spoken at the end of the seventh day. When she spoke, she sealed the destiny of the sacred village and all its inhabitants.

In the silence, her voice echoed to the deepest recesses of the council house.

"The strength and future of our people lies in the knowledge of our sacred ways. If this is lost, it is the end of hope for us in our time, and in the time of our children's children. We were chosen and placed here for this purpose, and we must do that for which we were born. For the sake of those yet to be, we must accept the offer of the Nunne'hi. The wisdom will live with us, preserved for all who come to seek it. We are chosen to hold it for the people of our blood, and for all who seek harmony in the years to come. For this purpose, we must be sealed apart from the world. Within this mountain, we will live as the invisible, immortal Nunne'hi…. Forever."

Not a sound could be heard when she sat down. No one stirred. The decision was made when the Ghigham spoke the final word. Now they must be still and wait for the end of their time in the world they knew and prepare to enter the land of the immortals.

The Ghigham quieted the urge to go outside and drink in the sight of Sha-cona-gee, the beloved Smoky Mountains beyond the village walls. The desire for one last look at home, and the hope that she would see Twisted Hair coming down the path, was almost too much to bear. She saw the same longing mirrored in the faces of all the people in the council house, but they remained motionless. They would obey. In this and all things, they walked the way of harmony. That was part of the sacred wisdom they held.

The war chief's defiant cry shattered the silence. "No. I will not hide in the land of the Nunne'hi while our people perish. I will stay where I'm needed and defend our home land. Who will stand with me against our enemy?"

Brave warriors took a final quick glance at beloved ones they would see no more. With no time for farewells they stood with the war chief. Ignoring voices that pleaded with them to stay, they rushed away from the safety of the council house to an unknown future beyond its walls.

***

With the sound of grating stone, the door closed behind the warriors, shutting off the voices that called them back. The ancient town of their ancestors remained long enough for one brief look, then a great wind swept down from the mountain. Cold as the heart of winter, it caught and held them like twigs in a whirlpool, then as suddenly as it came, it died away.

The warmth of late summer once more touched the land but nothing else was the same. The town of the wisdom keepers was gone from the land. The protecting palisade no longer encircled the place their home once stood. Where there were houses and gardens, the warriors saw nothing but a green valley stretching out to the bend of the river. The mound remained, but no council house stood on its summit, and no fire burned.

The encircling mountains looked unchanged, until they glanced toward the place of the Nunne'hi. Where they remembered the stone face of their mountain as a smooth featureless cliff, a form now protruded. As if half the council house merged with the mountain and turned to stone, it jutted out with permanence that only living rock possessed.

No sign of life remained. The voices of their loved ones silent, and the door to their world closed forever.

One thing remained from their past; the weapons they left on the rack outside the council house. For that small mercy, they thanked the Nunne'hi, then took up their arms and set off into the forest.

***

Inside the lodge, the people heard the roaring wind beyond the walls. It shook the council house, causing some of the little ones to cry out in fear. The wind died, and all was still.

Whispered voices asked, "When will they take us inside the mountain?"

The war chief's wife leapt to her feet. "I will stay here with my husband. I don't want to go into the world of the Nunne'hi without him."

The Ghigham went with her. Perhaps they could persuade the warriors to wait with them for the Nunne'hi. They looked for the war chief and his warriors, but they were nowhere to be seen. The village appeared unchanged. Nothing looked different than when the day began. Corn, squash, and beans awaited harvest in the field. Dogs napped in the sun and the town stood as it had for generations. The people wandered back to their houses, relieved to find them unchanged. The protecting wall encircled the mother town as it always had.

The Ghigham watched and said nothing. They would know soon enough. She lifted her eyes to the encircling mountains that rose beyond the wall, marking the edge of their world, and remembered the words of the Nunne'hi. "You will have all you see within the ring of the hills around the town."

The Nunne'hi spared them all that was most dear. Nothing beyond the ring of hills existed for them.

It was enough.

The Lost Mother Town.

 In a secluded cove in the foothills, Twisted Hair and Tsi-s-qua spread their blankets on the bare ground beside the trail and laid down to rest. Summer wore to a close, and already a chill tinged the evening. The boy slept lightly while Twisted Hair lay awake, impatient for the morning. One little hill town lay between him and the last leg of the journey back to the mother town. The breeze that whispered in the trees, picked up force and became a chilling wind. He drew his blanket closer. The voice that spoke in the wind left no room to resist. "Go home," it said.

With the call of the Nunne'hi ringing in his ears, Twisted Hair roused Tsi-s-qua from sleep and set out for home.

A full moon lit the path. They kept their sight on the distant shadows against the sky, the mountains of home. For two days, they walked, stopping only when exhaustion or hunger forced them to.

Evening of the second day found them topping the last hill on the trail leading to the mother town. They stopped, straining their eyes for smoke from the sacred fire. When they saw nothing, a thrill of fear urged them into a run. They entered the valley, but no shouts of welcome reached their ears, and no one ran to meet them. No dogs barked, and no children called out to them. Not even the smell of a town lingered in the clear air.

In dismay, they walked where gardens once grew and homes lined the path. Where were the fields of corn, beans and squash, and the people reaping the harvest? Where were the cooking fires? Not a trace of the mother town remained, and none of the people were there to tell them why.

A faint trace of a path led to the mound. They followed the path and climbed the mound. Where was the council house and the sacred fire?

A voice hailed them from below. "No one is left but us, and we are leaving," the war chief called "We are not needed here. Our people are gone from this world. The Nunne'hi took them into the mountain. We go to defend our land against the strangers who brought the end of our world."

"Where are our people?" Twisted Hair said. He called the woman's name, knowing she would be waiting for him.

The war chief gestured toward the stone face of the mountain of the Nunne'hi. "The ones you seek are inside. You are too late." Without another word, the warriors departed.

Twisted Hair turned to the Nunne'hi's mountain. The remembered rock face that separated their world from the land of mortals was changed. No longer smooth and featureless, it displayed a protrusion like half a council house jutting from the stone.

How could his people be inside this strange stone outcropping on the face of the cliff?

He and Tsi-s-qua descended the mound and made their way across the valley and up the side of the mountain until they stood at the base of the strange protrusion. Like the seven-sided lodge carved into the living stone, it was now part of the mountain. Not a sound broke the

66

stillness. They touched the stone, searching for a way inside. The war chief said all the people were there. Was the woman waiting for him inside?

No door, no crevice, not even a crack in the stone hinted at an entrance. A smooth seamless rock face with no way in or out rose before them. While the boy searched for a seam in the stone where the council house door should have been, Twisted Hair climbed up the side and made his way to the roof, seeking the opening where the smoke from the sacred fire rose for all the generations to see, since the mother town came into being. He sat beside what used to be the smoke hole. A darkened circle spread from the center, a mark left by the smoke? It felt warm against his palm.

Could it be true that the Nunne'hi took the Uku, the Ghigham and all the wise elders into their world? The woman who waited for him, waited there alone and he couldn't reach her. Grief seized him. Why would they call him home, only to take his people and leave him and the boy behind in a world where they had no home?

He called the woman's name, pleading with her to answer. His voice echoed off the hills, the only sound he heard. Not even a bird's song or a cricket's call broke the silence. This had become a place of the Nunne'hi, where no bird, animal or creeping thing ventured. It had the feel of the world of the immortals.

He cried out to the Nunne'hi, "Why did you call me home then close the way?"

No answer came. He sat alone on the cold stone, remembering the wisdom of the Ghigham who became his mother when he was alone, the power and kindness of the Uku and the gentleness of the people.

Remembering the woman who waited.

They were as lost to him as the old storyteller who left him alone on the trail.

To be sealed inside the world of the immortals, meant separation from the mortal world, never to return. He understood why they chose to leave the land of men. Inside the mountain, the knowledge they held could be preserved for generations yet to come. But what of the wisdom he alone carried. He knew many things even the wisest Keetoowah had not learned. Would the sacred wisdom in his stories be forgotten when he and Tsi-s-qua no longer walked the land?

A ray of hope broke through his despair when a drumbeat reached his ears, so faint he thought it only a memory. As he listened it grew louder, sounding the heartbeat of the earth through the stone. Voices from deep within the mountain rose in a new song. They sang a story of an ageless Twisted Hair who lived inside the town of the Keetoowah. While generations passed in the world outside, his people would remember him and wait for the time when he walked among them again. In the days of the children's children, the promise of his return would give them hope. When they faced their greatest peril, he would come with forgotten wisdom and awaken memories of sacred ways.

Was this why they called him home, to join the people in the hidden village and take his rightful place with the wisdom keepers? They promised him a place inside to wait until a time in the future when the descendants of the Ani'yun Wiya needed his stories to restore them to harmony.

He looked out at the mountains and valleys. The river wound past the great mound where the mother town once stood, and the mist rose as it always had, like the smoke from a thousand pipes. A bittersweet understanding dawned. Someday he would walk here again, but now he must leave it behind. Until then, he was home.

Tsi-s-qua sat before what had once been the doorway to the council house. With his head resting on his arms, he looked the image of lost hope. Twisted Hair called to him. He rose to his feet and climbed to sit beside Twisted Hair.

"Listen," Twisted Hair said.

Muted voices rose through the stone. A look of wonder crossed the boy's face.

A new song rose in volume, singing the song of the great Twisted Hair who would abide in the timeless land, to return to the mortal world in time of need.

"Will the Nunne'hi take us into the mountain?" the boy asked.

"Listen," Twisted Hair said again.

A new song came, sorrowful but filled with promise, a song of a boy who must take up the staff of the Twisted Hair and walk the land alone, telling the story of the sacred hidden town to their people.

Understanding dawned. "I must go alone," he said.

"You are now the storyteller who carries a message of hope, of the wisdom keepers who live within the mountain of the Nunne'hi, holding wisdom for all who find their way to Sha-cona-gee to listen to their song."

Tsi-s-qua said, "I will tell them of the Twisted Hair who will return when his people need him most."

"You have a new story to tell the people. In the dark days ahead, some will journey here and listen to the wisdom keepers and find hope. If only a few find their way, the knowledge of this sacred place will not be lost. The world beyond this mountain will change, but here, all will remain the same."

Tsi-s-qua tried to appear brave but his pallor and trembling betrayed him.

"You are young to take on such a heavy burden," Twisted Hair said, "but you are prepared. I saw the strength in you when I first plucked you from the tree where you perched like a little bird, escaping the flood that took your people. I called you Tsi-s-qua, for it meant Bird in my language, and claimed you for my mother's clan. In the years we traveled together you prepared to take up the staff of the storyteller. Your time has come, and your work lies ahead."

The song inside the mountain ended, and profound silence settled around them. The soft tread of moccasin clad feet announced the approach of a man. They watched him come nearer, aware that this was no mortal. The perfection and beauty of his face and form marked him as one of the Nunne'hi. He reached for the Twisted Hair's great totem staff. Twisted Hair surrendered it to him. The Nunne'hi turned to Tsi-s-qua and offered the staff to him.

The boy hesitated.

The Nunne'hi said, "Take it. It is yours to carry now. You are the storyteller. Go to your people who remain in the world. Tell them of the knowledge the Keetoowah hold within this mountain. Here, those who seek truth with a pure heart will find it. When you are old and tired, come back to this place to rest. We will be waiting for you."

Tsi-s-qua stood up and reached for the staff. He could not speak through his sorrow. The Nunne'hi guided them to the foot of the mountain then turned to the boy, placing a hand upon his heart. "Your path will be hard, but our gift to you is strength, courage and enough time in the world to do the work appointed to you."

The fear lessened in the Tsi-s-qua's eyes. The touch of the Immortal imparted strength and well-being, but it could not ease the sorrow of parting.

When Twisted Hair tried to comfort him, the boy said, "You made me your son when I had no father or mother. Will I ever see you again?"

The Nunne'hi answered for him. "A long time will pass before you can come here again. The gift of the Nunne'hi's touch is a lengthy life among men. Generations will be born and die before you grow old. When another storyteller is ready to take your place, we will call you home. Go, and take the story you are given, my son. Learn the stories that are new and bring them home when you return. They are part of the wisdom we hold."

Twisted Hair embraced the boy one last time and walked with the Nunne'hi into the stone.

***

For the briefest moment, Tsi-s-qua caught a glimpse of the familiar mother town inside the mountain. The Ghigham, the Uku, and the woman, welcomed Twisted Hair home. The image faded and only the cold stone remained.

He stood alone outside, in the world with no one to guide him on a journey through a changing world. He dried his tears and began twisting strands of his long hair into ropes, the way he watched Twisted Hair do for most of his life. When it was done, he took up the great totem staff of the Storyteller. It felt awkward in his hands, but he knew one day it would be as much a part of him as the long line of storytellers who carried it before. He lifted it as high as he could and felt the change come over him. He became the Twisted Hair with his work ahead of him. The world beyond the mountain of the Nunne'hi, held dangers no storyteller before him faced.

Tsi-s-qua, the storyteller, turned from the mountain and began his journey alone into a changing land to tell his new story of constant wisdom.

A New Story of Hope

 The staff weighed heavy in the new storyteller's hands. He paused atop the hill that looked down on the empty valley where the mother town used to be, and remembered his first glimpse of the mound, and the smoke that rose from the sacred fire. Only the mound remained. The faintest mark of a path traversed the length of the town and ended at the foot of the mound.

He turned away and traveled the mountain trail, beyond the foothills and into the valley, avoiding towns and travelers for the first part of his journey. In solitude, he prepared, remembering the stories the Twisted Hair told when they were alone with the elders.

Beside a river where he once camped with Twisted Hair, he lingered for a while. On a crisp late fall morning, he rose at sunrise and purified himself with smoke, then went to water in the clear cold shallows. The sharp edge of grief dulled, the memories of the Turtle People that haunted his dreams lessened. He sat beside his fire and recalled all the stories. In them he found the key to mysteries that restored him to harmony and taught him to claim his inheritance.

Alone, in the forest with only memories to guide him, he became the new Twisted Hair, and understood why he survived when all his people drowned. This was his story, his part of the legacy of holy men who held the memory of his people. The thought filled him with purpose. When he took up the great staff, it fit the curve of his hand and felt lighter when he lifted it high.

With new confidence, he set out on the trail.

When a voice challenged him from the forest, he stopped and lifted the staff of the storyteller in greeting, remembering how the people rejoiced when they saw Twisted Hair raise it.

The warriors who stepped out onto the trail circled him. There was no welcome in their greeting. "Where is the Twisted Hair," they asked.

"He is gone from this world," Tsi-s-qua said. "I bring a new story he sends to you from the mountain of the Nunne'hi."

Still cautious, they took him to their town. The chief saw the staff and asked, "How did the Twisted Hair meet his fate? Was he taken by the Turtle People?"

"He still lives," the storyteller said. "But he is not in this world. He lives in the mountain of the Nunne'hi with the Keetoowah and all the people of the mother town. There they hold the wisdom of our sacred ways."

The chief sent his wife to prepare food and lodging. "This is a story for all the elders to hear," the chief said. "Rest now, and we will listen when they are gathered."

When night fell, the new storyteller stood before the people. For the first time, he told of the hidden mother town inside the Nunne'hi's mountain. He sang the song he heard, rising through the stone of the council house, of a holy man who waited within until his people called him in a time of great peril. The song ended with the promise that Twisted Hair would return when his people needed him most and bring the stories that saved them.

They listened, confused and sorrowful that the Twisted Hair they knew was lost to them.

"Where are all the people of the mother town? Where are the Keetoowah who know the sacred ways?" they asked.

Tsi-s-qua, the storyteller revealed to them the promise of the Keetoowah. "They still live in the world of the Nunne'hi where they will speak to all who come in a sacred manner and listen."

"The world of the Nunne'hi is hidden from us. How do we find our way to the place where the Keetoowah keep the wisdom?" they asked.

Tsi-s-qua told them of the mound that still stood, and the trail across the mountain, to the place where the mother town used to be. "Stand upon the sacred mound and look to the mountain. You will know it by the stone outcrop that looks like half a seven-sided council house."

While the elders discussed who among them must go to seek the mountain of the Nunne'hi, Tsi-s-qua listened, pleased that the first telling of the new story brought worthy seekers who would travel to find the council house inside the mountain.

He departed the town and traveled into a fearful world with his legend of a place where the Keetoowah preserved the wisdom for generations yet to come. Many towns still flourished, untouched by the invading strangers, but wary of their approach.

As he traveled farther from home, he came upon devastated towns and villages where the strangers swept through, leaving a hopeless remnant of the people. He gave them the only hope he could offer, his story of a holy man who would come in times of trouble, telling stories and teaching the sacred ways.

Those who despaired, fearing they would not endure long enough to see the day of Twisted Hair's return, took heart when Tsi-s-qua told them of the place in the mountains where the Keetoowah held wisdom, it gave them comfort to know all was not lost.

Word of his story preceded him, and Tsi-s-qua found welcome in every town he entered. Everywhere he went he prepared the way for the return of Twisted Hair.

They asked him when the great holy man would come again. The storyteller looked into the distance and said softly, "I do not know." In his heart, he hoped it would be soon.

Years passed, and still he walked the land alone. The memory of the mound shaped like a seven-sided council house gave him courage. There, the wisdom keepers lived.

Tsi-s-qua's knowledge grew, for he fulfilled the duty laid on him by the Nunne'hi to learn from the people and bring new stories with him when he came home to the mountain. He held every story in his heart to add to the store amassed by the Keetoowah who preserved the wisdom of the people.

His travels with the Twisted Hair prepared him to become the storyteller everyone welcomed. He knew the stories told around the fire to all who listened, and the sacred chronicles revealed to none but the wisest elders in the villages.

The elders understood when he told them of the mountain where the wisdom keepers waited in the hidden village. When he told them to send their worthy seekers to listen for their voices, they chose a few of the wisest to journey to that holy place.

The years wore on, and Tsi-s-qua left behind the insecurities of youth and became a man. His twisted hair grew long, adorned with precious stones and silver beads, gifted from the people who listened to his stories. His travels took him across the land, through towns that still stood strong, and villages ravaged by the encroaching strangers. The hardship gave him a strong body and clear visage. He saw the eyes of the women on him, and there were times he found comfort and companionship, but only for a short while. The trail lay always before him, and he traveled it alone.

A winter came when snow obstructed the trails. He lodged in a town of long houses beside a lake, resting from his travels. A woman, strong and wise, led the people and joined the warriors in battle when enemies came. She listened to his stories with the elders who lingered by the fire and understood the deep wisdom within them.

On cold evenings Tsi-s-qua watched other men go to their homes with little ones and their mother and felt the depth of solitude that lay ahead for him. When the evening fires burned low, loneliness cut to the bone.

A wintry night found him restless, rising from his bed to walk on a snowy hillside near the town. A lone figure silhouetted against the light of the full moon caught his eye. Long hair loosened from their braids, flowed in the brisk wind. The headwoman lifted her face to the sky, looking to the moon. He watched and could almost feel the burden of responsibility she bore. Without a word, he went to stand beside her.

"Strange men came to our town and offered to trade for hides," she said. "Some of the men want to do as they ask. They will trade beaver skins for weapons like the strangers use."

"The strangers offer friendship and trade, but they bring death," the storyteller said. He had seen it in other towns.

"Their weapons are more powerful than ours," she said. "How can I say no, if the trade might save us? With weapons that match theirs, we could stand against the enemy who comes to fight."

"Do you want to trade with the strangers, when you know the harm they do to our people?"

She didn't answer. He understood her quandary. Her warriors faced defeat if they went against the strangers with bows and spears. Their weapons gave her people a chance, but she couldn't trust the strangers.

"What will you do?" he asked.

"Hunters are already taking skins to trade. They are defying the council. Some of them even now have guns and are learning from the strangers how to use them."

He had seen it before. The strangers caused dissention among the people. They pitted warriors against chiefs, and the cautious against the foolhardy. Harmony failed when the strangers came. He stood beside her and looked down at the peaceful longhouses in the snow. Generations lived and died in the town and knew peace. With a clarity that wounded him to the core, he saw it coming to an end. Even when they came in peace, to trade or talk, the strangers brought dissention.

He moved closer to her, sharing his warmth. "It is true, they can't be defeated without better weapons, but to trade with them will be the downfall of your town. Greed will take root here, and greed is more powerful than fear when threat comes with a kind face."

She rested her head on his shoulder. He spread his blanket around her and the night felt warmer. The world changed around them, and peril in many forms approached, but in the moonlight, they were no longer alone. With a full heart, he went with the headwoman to her lodge.

Winter came to an end, and the trail called. The headwoman walked with him to the hillside on the edge of town to bid him farewell. She didn't ask him to stay. She understood duty. He promised to come back to her, then watched her walk away, tall and proud, to lead her people through the tough times ahead.

He continued his journey, holding in his heart the memory of the winter he spent with her, and the trail felt less lonely.

He lost count of the seasons that passed, and still he journeyed telling his story of the Ghigham, the Uku, and the healing village that disappeared into myth long ago. The Nunne'hi's gift of long life, allowed him to see many changes and grieve the death of many friends

Even when the legend became well known, he repeated it. The healing village and the Keetoowah who waited there came to life in his stories. They lived with the immortals inside their mountain, always waiting, and always wise. In time, his story became so well known the young repeated the promise when he ended it. "The Twisted Hair lives in the mountain of the Nunne'hi, but when we need him most, he will come back to us."

In every town, a few lingered late into the night and asked, "How can I find the mountain of the Nunne'hi?" Tsi-s-qua told them of Sha-cona-gee, the Mountains Covered with Smoke, and the stone that protruded from the mountain in the shape of a seven-sided council house.

In time, the story included the tale of the a few brave seekers who found the mountain and listened. When they came in a sacred manner and waited in silence, they heard the song of the wisdom keepers. There, in the stillness of a hidden place in Sha-cona-gee, the Keetoowah sang for the sake of the children's children. They brought the story home, and the people remembered.

When Tsi-s-qua heard this, it lightened his spirit and made his long journey worthwhile.

Throughout the land, he traveled while the years passed. A few times he made his way back to the town of long houses, to the head woman who waited for him. Trouble came to her people as he knew it would. They used their trade weapons to hunt more animals just for the hides the strangers craved. Food became scarce, and harmony among the people frayed. The strangers brought poison that robbed the men of reason and left their women and children hungry. The fiery drink cost more hides than the weapons, and further decimated the forest.

On his final journey to her town, he found her tired and broken. She sat alone in her lodge, weary of fighting a losing battle. The strangers didn't attack her town as they did others. There, the destruction was more insidious. The longhouses, once warm and well maintained, stood rundown and neglected. Lost and dispirited people greeted him with a halfhearted attempt at an almost forgotten formality.

He stayed with the head woman, willing her to find the strength to come with him, knowing she would not leave her people. On a dark night when the snow fell on the hill, she walked with him one last time. He caught her up in his arms when she faltered, and watched the spirit leave her as she walked away from this world. With her body lying beneath the hill, he left her town never to return. They had no use for his stories there, and it held nothing but sorrow for him.

The years passed, and grief dulled. While the touch of the Nunne'hi made his life longer than other men, age marked him on the evening he entered a silent town in the lowlands. Tired and lonely, he hoped for a winter's rest with people who sheltered him in other cold seasons.

This time, old friends did not come to meet him on the path, no welcoming voices reached his ears. Even when he walked among the lodges, no one called his name.

This was not the first town where only empty lodges and silence greeted him, but the heartache never lessened. Memories of old friends haunted every shadow. An old man and woman who sheltered him last winter, lay dead at their door. Everywhere he looked, only the dead remained.

He could not dig graves in the frozen ground, so he did the only thing he could to honor the spirits of the departed. One by one he carried them to the shell of a house at the edge of the town. He brought wood from the ruins for fuel and cedar branches for purity and set the fire.

The cold winds that blew across the hills promised snow by nightfall. The chill cut him to the quick and his body ached with fatigue. He returned to the house where he stayed before when grief and exhaustion rendered him unable to travel to the next town. He placed his pack and the totem staff of the Twisted Hair inside the house. He brought wood to the asi beside it for a fire and placed smooth round stones in the flames.

When the fire burned down to coals and the stones glowed red, he poured a pot of water on the heated stones and steam filled the asi. He sat naked while hot steam pulled the ache and fatigue from his body and eased the sorrow in his heart. Wrapped in his blanket beside the remnants of the fire, he passed a restless night filled with dreams and voices from the past.

Morning broke gray and cold. Tsi-s-qua surfaced reluctantly from a dream that took him back to the boy he used to be. The voice of Twisted Hair still echoed in his head, bringing that day to his memory, reminding him how afraid and alone he felt clinging to the tree while the water surged beneath him. Remembered fear cut sharp as a knife as he watched the flood take his people leaving him alone in the world. He could almost hear the muddy water rushing below him, sweeping away everything in its path.

He awoke with the voice of the Twisted Hair echoing in his mind, telling him to remember how he felt as a child without mother or father, alone in the world. And the relief that came when the holy man plucked him from the tree and carried him away.

Unable to sleep, he rose and climbed a hill near the village. He greeted the sun and offered prayers to Creator. The dream lingered in his mind. Why did the Twisted Hair awaken an old and painful memory?

In the stillness, he heard the soft cry of a child, quickly muffled by his mother's hand. He followed the sound to a crevice under the hill.

There, he found a woman cowering in fright, clutching her little son to her breast. The fear in her eyes turned to hope when she saw him. She led the child into the sunlight and looked back at the ruin that was her home. "We must search for anyone who is left alive," she said.

"There is no one," Tsi-s-qua told her.

She wept softly as she told him how she fled with her youngest son when the strangers came to raid the village. Hiding in the only place she could find, she listened to the cries of her people, afraid the strangers would find her and take her only son. Not all were killed, she told him, just the sick and old. The rest were rounded up to be sold as slaves. Many died trying to get away. She saved one son, but two others and their father stood with the warriors against the strangers.

This was not a new story. The strangers saw the people of the land as a resource to harvest, and healthy young slaves brought profit.

He gave the woman the only solace he had to give. "Your people who died, were honored with prayers and death songs. Their bodies are joined with the earth through fire. No more harm can come to them. Their spirits are free. We must go now. More will come to seek plunder in the empty lodges."

She went with him to retrieve his pack from the ruined town and wept when she saw the vacant lodges and blood-stained snow. She gathered up a blanket and one lone child's shirt in her house and turned her eyes to the trail.

The storyteller whistled, and a dark little mare came cantering to his side. He received few gifts from the people now, for they had little to give. In a town on the grasslands, a warrior who traveled to the mountain and listened, gave him a horse won from a stranger in battle. The mother feared the horse. She had never been near one before, but she let him help her mount it.

With the child in his arms and the woman clinging to his waist, he rode away, saving them from the fate suffered by most of the people in her town.

They traveled North up the course of a creek staying close to its banks. The woman rode in silence, refusing food when he offered, and speaking only to her son to sooth him when he cried. The storyteller remembered when he was a boy locked in silence, too filled with anguish to speak, and how the Twisted Hair cared for him until he healed.

In three days, they came to a village too small to be noticed by the strangers. The people of the town welcomed them and cared for the woman through the winter. When they gathered around the fire on cold evenings to listen to his stories, the woman's child sat close by the storyteller's side. With his eyes closed, the boy sat so still he seemed to be asleep, but he was listening. Tsi-s-qua observed and knew the boy heard each word and held it in his heart, for he had done the same so many years ago, as he sat beside the Twisted Hair. With the resilience of the very young, the boy thrived in the town. He formed bonds with the people and found friends among the other boys, but Tsi-s-qua was the one he came to at end of day. His mother saw and was grateful. She called her son Sope. In her tongue, it meant Only Son, for he was the only one of her children the strangers left to her. Sadness never left her eyes and each day found her more frail and weak.

A fever came upon her in the dead of winter. Weakened by grief, she lacked the strength to heal. On a night, when she could no longer rise from her bed, she called Tsi-s-qua to her side and begged him to take care of her son. When he gave her his word, she kissed little Sope for the last time and closed her eyes.

They buried the woman under an oak tree beside the creek, wrapped in the blanket she saved from her house. Sope sat by her grave through the night and wept. Tsi-s-qua stayed with him and remembered his mother who had no grave.

When Tsi-s-qua rode away in the spring, Sope went with him. The storyteller thought of the Twisted Hair who took him when he was a boy without mother or father.

The journey was less lonely now.

84

His heart grew lighter as they traveled together through the land. Sope asked about the stories as he sat easily astride the mare. His questions illustrated how much he learned, and how well he understood the wisdom held in the heart of the stories. Even the deeper legends the elders told captivated him. He learned to recite them, word for word, precisely the same each time, the way they came down from the ancestors.

The storyteller's spirit was at peace. When the time came to go back to the mountain, Sope would be ready to take his place.

The years passed, and the dark little mare no longer traveled with him. When her old bones needed rest, she stayed behind to live out her days with the honor due a horse who carried a holy man on his travels. The young men of the town replaced her with two strong, white stallions taken from the strangers, and a sturdy young pony that carried their packs. It made their travels easier.

The trail punished his body, worn by a life that spanned many generations. In the quiet of the night, he listened to the wind. When would the voices under the mountain call him home? Even a man touched by the Nunne'hi's hand, must reach the end of his time in the world. He sometimes kept silent around the fires and let Sope tell the stories. Sope became a strong young man, well-loved by the people and accepted as the next Twisted Hair. They could see the years bear down on Tsi-s-qua. When he told of the hidden mother town under the mountain of the Nunne'hi, and the Twisted Hair who waited there for him, he couldn't hide the longing in his eyes.

Harvest time approached when the voices at last spoke in the wind. First the Nunne'hi, then the Twisted Hair.

"Your work is done Tsi-s-qua. Come home."

He said to Sope, "It is time for you to see the place where the wisdom keepers wait. There you will learn many things I cannot teach you." He couldn't bear to tell him this would be their last journey together.

They traveled inland toward the highlands, keeping to the forests and away from places where the strangers lived. When they lodged in the towns of his people, Tsi-s-qua sat by the fires with the elders and sometimes told his stories. More often, he listened with pride while Sope took the role he would soon fill alone.

Late summer found them deep in the mountains on a wide path covered with pine needles. Climbing down from his horse he walked, as he did the first time he traveled the trail to the mother town. The path felt soft under foot. At the foot of the hill, he paused. Did he imagine the faint scent of cooking fires that promised a feast to come? Muted voices drifted across the valley from the mountain.

"The Storyteller is coming."

He rounded the mound that once rose above the mother town. "This is where the mother town once stood," he told Sope. "Atop this mound stood the council house where the sacred fire burned."

Again, voices called from the mountain, growing louder, "Tsi-s-qua, the storyteller is coming."

He pointed to the outcropping on the side of the mountain. Trees grew high around the stone lodge. Vines trailed across it leaving only an outline to mark where it stood.

"There, you can still see the image of the council house. Inside the mountain, Twisted Hair and the wisdom keepers hold the wisdom and sacred ways of our people. All I have learned will soon be added to the store of knowledge."

Sadness clouded Sope's face as understanding dawned. Without a word, he followed Tsi-s-qua to the end of their last journey together. His steps slowed as they neared the mountain.

"When will you leave me?" Sope asked.

"Not until you are ready," Tsi-s-qua said. "We must climb up to the council house and wait for the story they will give you."

His eagerness to hear the Keetoowah speak vied with his sorrow at the thought of parting, but Sope tempered his emotions and looked to the storyteller for guidance. He had learned well that a holy place must be approached in a sacred manner.

Sope built a small fire. Tsi-s-qua took sage and cedar from his pack and gave it to Sope and the young man mixed it in a bowl, then lit it with a glowing ember from the fire. A rich, fragrant smoke rose from the mixture. Soap chanted a prayer as he swirled the smoke around Tsi-s-qua, then allowed the storyteller to use the smoking bowl to purify him in turn. When the smoke cleansed them, they laid offerings of wild tobacco at the base of the mountain then climbed up to council house.

On the cold smooth stone, beside the place where the fire from the sacred fire once rose, they sat, waiting.

"Be still and listen," the storyteller said. "You will hear a new story that you alone must take to the people."

Together they waited for voices to speak from beneath the stone

In the silence, they heard no birdsong, no rustling of insect or animals for this was a place of the Nunne'hi. No living thing intruded where they lived.

87

It began with a distant drumbeat vibrating through the stone. Voices joined the drums in a song of welcome and blessing. One by one the voices faded away until only one remained. In somber tones, it sang about a changing world and what it would become in the time of the new storyteller. No Twisted Hair before had faced so great a peril, or such an alien land, and Sope must face it alone. Tsi-s-qua would no longer travel with him.

Tsi-s-qua waited by Sope's side through the day, watching while Sope learned the story he must take to the people. Anguish settled over the young man's features as he listened.

Evening came, and the song continued. Voices sang of loneliness and duty, of heartbreaking changes to the homeland of his people. Sope trembled but didn't turn away. He sat still and took it all in, holding every word in his heart. He learned from Tsi-s-qua to be faithful to the story, just the way it came to him.

Among the voices that spoke to Sope, one quietly called to Tsi-s-qua

"Welcome home."

That single voice rose above the rest. "Welcome home, my son. Your work is done"

His heart danced with the beat of the drum, but he would not join Twisted Hair yet. He waited with Sope, watching him rise to stand tall and proud and begin twisting strands of his hair. Peace came to Tsi-s-qua spirit. The work of the Twisted Hair would go on as it had through all the days of their people. Sope's life as the holy man who kept the stories would begin when he left the mountain, and end when he came home, leaving another to take his place.

With long ropes of hair bound with beaded thongs at his crown, Sope joined an unbroken line of holy men who held the mysteries and wisdom of the people. He understood from the Keetoowah's song that he faced a hard and friendless journey, yet he took on the mantle of the storyteller without flinching.

He faced Tsi-s-qua with unshed tears glistening in his eyes at the thought of parting.

The storyteller embraced him and said, "Go, my son. Tell the people we are here. When you are old and tired, come back to this mountain and you will find your well-earned rest. I will be waiting."

Tsi-s-qua raised the great totem staff one last time, a salute to the world he left behind, and passed it on to Sope, the next Twisted Hair.

Sope's hands shook when he lifted its weight for the first time. The honor and burden of the great staff of the Twisted Hair was his to bear now.

Tsi-s-qua saw the change that came over him when he raised it high.

The same Nunne'hi, who bestowed long life on Tsi-s-qua so long ago, appeared beside them as silently as he came in the past. With no word of greeting, he placed his hand on Sope's heart and gave him the gift that allowed him to remain in the mortal world beyond the appointed days of a human being. Sope understood. Tsi-s-qua prepared him for this moment.

The storyteller watched the Nunne'hi bestow his blessing, anxious to turn his duties over to Sope. The voice he waited so long to hear, called from the open door below.

Twisted Hair emerged and lifted his arms in welcome, little changed from when they parted so long ago. The only mark of age was a touch of grey among his twisted strands of hair.

They embraced, and the years fell away. The storyteller looked through the wall of stone and saw a place long passed from the world. Unchanged faces from a time long ago smiled welcome. Old friends ran to meet him while familiar voices called him home.

"The storyteller has come."

He lifted his head and began to sing an old song that honored the ancestors, the first to light the sacred fire.

Tsi-s-qua, the storyteller was home, bringing stories of the people.

Unto These Hills

 The Nunne'hi's hand lingered over Sope's heart, bestowing the blessing of the immortals on the new storyteller. With infinite sadness, Sope watched the Nunne'hi follow Tsi-s-qua and Twisted Hair through the stone. For one brief instant, Sope took in the sight of the fabled mother town, then nothing remained but emptiness. Vines trailed across the face of the cliff and trees grew near the outcropping. Only someone who knew what to seek, would know what they concealed.

Sope stood alone and afraid. How could he go forth with nothing but a story of ruin and sorrow? The Keetoowah's song showed him images of loss and despair, without a single morsel of hope to give the people reason to endure? It was more than he could bear.

He climbed to the top of top of the council house stone and waited, pleading for something to soften the dread the story the Keetoowah foretold.

Soft voices responded, urging him to be strong, that he could come home to the mountain when his work was done.

He called out to those inside the mound, "But what of the people who suffer at the hands of the strangers? Where is their safety? What can I tell them that will give them solace?"

The voices sang again and still the song held visions of things too dreadful to endure. His heart ached, but he did not turn away. The songs prepared him for the desolation to come and helped him understand that nothing could turn it aside. He listened until the song ended, leaving images of devastation lingering in his mind.

"What can I do to lessen the pain of our people in the evil days to come?" he asked. "If it must come to past, how can I give them the strength to endure?"

No words of comfort came from the voices within the mound. No hint of anything that would spare the people or comfort them in the days ahead.

He could not walk among his people with only stories of doom and hopelessness. In all the myths, he knew, some ray of light pierced the darkness, some answer lay within the legend. He lay face down on the cold stone, pleading with the unseen Nunne'hi for something to ease the despair his story visited upon the people.

In the unbroken silence, he waited for a reply that didn't come. He called out to the wisdom keepers, but his call went unanswered.

Alone atop the council house stone, he watched the sun set behind the mountains. The full moon rose and shimmered off the mist, and still he watched. Without food or drink, he kept his vigil.

On the third night, his strength deserted him, and he fell asleep. Vivid dreams came at once, a visual retelling of what he already knew. He saw the Ani'yun Wiya dressed in rags, walking through an icy rain that froze the ground and turned to ice in their threadbare clothing. They looked back at the valleys and mountains formed by the wings of Grandfather Buzzard and wept.

He watched them walk a long hard trail marked with shallow graves. Grief etched its mark on every face, but the dead were not their deepest sorrow. They had lost the homeland; the very flesh and bones of the ancestors. In Sha-cona-gee lingered the spirits that empowered holy people to keep the sacred ways and hold harmony in the world. There lay secret places where invisible immortals watched over them. In the deep forests, Awi Usdi and his people roamed, and unseen doorways marked entrances to the world of the immortals. Little people no longer danced in the clearings but retreated to the safety of lands beyond the houses of the strangers.

Sope saw it all taken away. He watched the Ani'yun-Wiya suffer on a long, forced march that took them far away from the Smoky Mountains and valleys of Sha-cona-gee.

From the depths of despair came his cry. "Is there no shred of comfort I can offer?"

Again, a vision stirred before him. He saw a strange man in a long black coat, kneeling on the ground at the head of a great procession of his people. Pale strangers stood nearby with their weapons. The man in black lifted his hands toward the sky and began to speak in a loud voice. *"I will lift up mine eyes unto these hills from whence comes my help."*

The people listened with downcast eyes while he read from his book. Then, one of the strangers shouted a command and fired his weapon. Whips cracked, and wagons filled with people lurched forward. Children and elders shed silent tears as they looked back on the misty mountains and valleys of home, knowing they would never see them again.

A few of the people rode horses, but most walked, bowed down by sadness. A bitter wind tore autumn's last brown and gold leaves from ancient trees. Needles of icy rain added to misery already beyond bearing.

The people looked back in sorrow for a while, then turned their faces west to the trail ahead. The Ani'yun Wiya were leaving Sha-cona-gee, but the man in black promised them hope would come from the hills. It wasn't much, but it gave him something to cling to on the journey.

At sunrise Sope woke from his dreams and took up the totem staff of the Twisted Hair. He could learn no more from the wisdom keepers. Their voices no longer rose through the stone. With sorrow like a weight on his soul he pitied those who must wait helplessly beneath the mountain of the Nunne'hi. It was Sope's fate to suffer with his people while the devastation they foretold came to pass, but the Keetoowah could only wait and grieve the suffering of their people.

He was no longer young when he rode away. The Nunne'hi's touch could keep his body strong and youthful for generations, but the visions they showed him aged his spirit. Knowing there was nothing he could do to turn aside what lay ahead, he set forth to face it, setting a straight course to the place where his destiny as the storyteller began.

He felt the need to pay honor to his mother beside her grave before he began the journey the Keetoowah set for him.

In the little village by the creek, he drew strength from the comfort of old friends and rested for a while. When he told his story around the evening fire, he held back nothing. His words painted pictures of sorrow so deep, it wounded the very land. The elders wept but young men spoke with courage of how they would assemble warriors from other tribes and stand together with them against the strangers. No enemy could defeat them if they banded together.

In sadness, he listened and said nothing. If brave talk could give them hope, it was more than he could offer.

He encouraged them with stories of other courageous men and women who would help them keep a remnant of their people alive. He had seen it in his visions on the mound. There would be a few who remained among the hills of home to hold their spirit in the land. Everything would not be lost. *"I will lift up mine eyes unto the hills from whence comes my help,"* the man in black said. The Council House on the mountain was in the hills of home, and the wisdom keepers inside offered hope, but there would be others in Sha-cona-gee to render aid. The man in black promised it. The homeland of the Ani'yun-Wiya would be lost, but not forever.

He told them of the man dressed in black. The words he spoke confused them, but they would remember: *"I will lift up my eyes unto these hills from whence comes my help."*

Before he left the little village by the river, he carried stones to his mother's grave and built a mound over her bones. His vision showed him a day when no trace of the town remained. Perhaps a mound of stone would weather the years to mark the place where he always came when he craved the feel of home.

He knew from the visions, there would be nothing else.

Kanagwa'ti

 A lone house sat in the clearing at the bottom of the hill. An Ani'yun Wiya village once spread out over the valley below, filling it with the sight and sounds of life. Twisted Hair remembered how the people rushed out to greet him when he last stood on the hilltop. No one welcomed him this time. His people were gone, and the strangers lived there now. Many years had passed since he last came this way. Now, he did not come as the storyteller. Another carried the great staff and walked the land. A young man named Sope.

He turned away and traveled along the ridge, back into the forest.

Two women waited among the trees, his guides through the trackless wilderness where the strangers didn't venture. He carried a treasure in his pack they would take if they could. The trail he traveled long ago, held new dangers that didn't exist when he walked it before.

Twisted Hair and the women kept to the thickets and deep woods, avoiding settlers and travelers. The gift of the Uku must be kept safe until he delivered it into the hands of the man the Nunne'hi trusted to use it well and protect it from those who would misuse it. Perhaps with the power it gave him, he could hold a small place for the Ani'yun Wiya in the sacred land.

The women who guided him did not need a path. Through pathless woods and hills, they set a rapid pace. When night came, they watched while Twisted Hair slept through the darkness, then woke him at day break to continue the journey. The rough terrain and tireless pace posed no hardship for him. Though a few strands of silver threaded through his twisted hair, his body was still young, and stronger than when he last journeyed through these lands.

At the edge of the forest, a river cut through the valley and around green hills. They ventured beyond the cover of a spruce grove to look down at a strange town of rough houses. Men shouted to each other in the muddy streets. Twisted Hair traveled among the tribes of all the land, learning the tongues of many people but the language of these men was strange to him.

He didn't need to understand their words to know this place held danger for him and the Uku's gift. They turned back to the cover of the forest but not before a pale man on horseback rode through the trees and saw them. He whipped his horse into a run and came at them with his weapon drawn.

The women urged Twisted Hair to run but he held back. He could not leave them to face the stranger alone. One of them pulled him away, leaving the other to hold off the attacker. He protested, until the woman reminded him of the value of what he carried in his pack and the strength of the woman they left behind. A Nunne'hi woman had nothing to fear from a mortal man. The bearded, pale skinned man would soon find himself greatly outmatched.

She caught up with them before they were out of sight, unharmed by her encounter.

The second day's journey brought them to their destination, an Ani'yun Wiya village hidden deep in the Smoky Mountains. The two women vanished into the forest and left him to enter alone.

He approached the walled village and stood at the entrance, waiting for an invitation to enter. Sentries watched atop the wall. Where were the cries of welcome that greeted him when he came to a town? The gate opened enough for two warriors with lances to come through. More armed men stood guard behind them, denying him entry. He spoke in their tongue and told them his name. In disbelief, the warriors stepped aside, and then followed him into the narrow twisting entry.

A warrior called aloud, "He is come. The one who was promised is here."

When he came inside, and they saw him, the people erupted in a welcome more fitting for a holy man. He heard the cry announcing his arrival, "The Twisted Hair has come."

They dropped everything and gathered around him, their eyes alight with reverent awe. They touched his garments and wondered at their richness.

A grandfather, his eyes dimmed with age, reached out to touch the twisted strands of his hair. "Another storyteller came here many seasons ago. He had a simple name and told of a hidden town where the old ones wait to speak. He said a great Twisted Hair lived there and would come to us in times of need."

They offered food, the best of all they had, but he refused. The smell from the cooking fires tempted him, but he would not eat yet. His fast began the day he left the hidden village in preparation for what he came to do and must continue until it was done.

He asked them to take him to the man the Nunne'hi found worthy. Kanagwa'ti, he was called. The Water Moccasin.

"He is an outsider," the elder said. "Not one of the Ani'yun Wiya. But he is a man of courage and wisdom who honors the ways of our people,"

They took him to the house of Kanagwa'ti. The young outsider welcomed him to lodge with him and his Ani'yun Wiya wife.

When they were alone, Kanagwa'ti asked, "Why have you come? We have been told you would return when our peril was greatest. Do you come to warn us? Can you tell us how to fight our enemy?"

Twisted Hair said, "I have come to find the only one who is strong and pure enough to use an ancient power to help our people. With it, he will assure that a place is held for us in this land."

Kanagwa'ti asked questions that only a wise man would know to ask. "What is the peril we face, and how will the chosen one overcome it?" Though the answers Twisted Hair gave him were strange and terrible, he listened.

"When you find the one to whom you will entrust this gift of power, I will be at his right hand," Kanagwa'ti said.

"You are the one I seek," Twisted Hair said. "You will be trusted with great power and a terrible burden and you must bear it alone."

Kanagwa'ti drew a deep breath, and composed himself, then asked, "What must I do?"

"You must learn how to use the gift you will receive. Understand its story and what it can do. There is great danger if it is used unwisely, so you must protect it and never allow it to fall into the wrong hands. Keep it in secret until you place it in the care of someone you trust, when it's time for you to walk over to the next world. If you use it rightly, you can save our people. If you are weak, you will be a part of their destruction. You can refuse if you wish, but you must do it now. Once it is in your hands, it will be too late to turn aside."

Kanagwa'ti paled. "How do I prepare?" he asked.

"We will go to a place apart where you will learn the secrets of the Uku. For seven days, you will not take food or drink. After your purification, you will receive the gift sent to you by a holy man who left the world long ago. The Nunne'hi searched for the one who was worthy, and they found you. You are Suye'ta, the chosen one."

In silence, they watched the sun set behind mountains.

"I am ready," Kanagwa'ti said.

"Tomorrow, we begin," Twisted Hair said.

With the lighting of evening fires, drumbeats called the Ani'yun Wiya together. They gathered in the circle of firelight and waited for the holy man. A rush of excitement ran through the crowd when Twisted Hair made his way to the fireside and lifted his hand in greeting. They hung on every word when he told the old stories passed down through the generations. Some, they knew, but many were forgotten. He was a legend come to life, and they listened in awe.

He told them of the mother town in the bend of the river, and of the wise Keetoowah who lived there. "A seven-sided council house sat atop a mound in the middle of town. Inside, the sacred fire burned unquenched through the years, a symbol of the unity and harmony of our people. There, the spirit of our people was strong, and the knowledge gained by our ancestors was kept alive and taught to the young. When we reclaim the sacred ground where our ancestors lived, and rekindle the sacred fire, our strength will return, and once again we will be the people of the one fire."

They knew of the mother town, but not where to find it. "The strangers have claimed much of the land where our people once lived," the chief said. "The mother town is lost to us."

"Tell us of the mother town," an elder said.

Twisted Hair made the mother town live once more in his stories for it was still his home. There in the mountain of the Nunne'hi, it stood as it always had. The Ghigham, the Uku, and the woman who waited for him, remained unchanged.

"The mother town is gone from this world and the place where it stood, is lost," he said, "but a time will come when the ancestors will reveal the mound where the sacred fire burned, and the place where the Keetoowah lived in the ancient home of our people. In that day, the children's children will come home to learn of the sacred ways of the first people who kindled the fire that united our people in harmony."

Late into the night, the people listened and asked questions. His answers revealed the deepest meaning of the old stories and helped them understand the wisdom hidden within them, buried treasure to give them pride in the legacy they inherited from the old ones.

His stories restored their lost heritage, brought forgotten wisdom to mind, and instilled in them the courage to endure through the dark days ahead. A new spirit came to the people of the village that night.

Kanagwa'ti sat in silence, attending to every word. Twisted Hair saw, and it pleased him. The wisdom of his ancestors was all he could offer to ease the burden of the Uku's gift.

A holy man sat by Kanagwa'ti's side. Twisted Hair asked him if he remembered the story of Uktena and the Ulunsu-ti.

"The Ulunsu-ti was lost long ago," The holy man said. He went on to tell of the story of the great serpent and the fear he brought to the land. He praised the warrior who defeated the serpent and claimed the Ulunsu-ti, using it for the good of his people.

Twisted Hair found comfort in the reverence the holy man showed for the ancestor who slew the Uktena and used the crystal to protect the people. He knew the good the Ulunsu'ti could do in the right hands, and the wrong that could come from its misuse. He would be an immense help to the outsider.

A few others remembered the story but thought it only a myth to entertain the children.

"There is wisdom even in the myths we tell the children," the holy man said.

Twisted Hair shifted the deerskin pouch across his shoulder as if it weighed heavy on his back. He stood and waited for silence. One more story he must tell before he left with the outsider to begin his preparation.

The people around the fire gathered closer, waiting for the story to begin.

Twisted Hair said, "Remember this, tell it to the children and keep it for the generations yet to come." Every eye was on him as he unfolded a mystery.

"In the long-ago times, the ancestors of the Ani'yun Wiya made their home in these mountains called Shacona-gee. Where the smoke of the first people still lingers, they planted the three sisters, corn, beans and squash, and the earth provided.

In the land far to the north, the people knew only war. Each man's hand was lifted against his brother and no tribe was friend to any other. There the chiefs became thirsty for the blood of their enemies, and all men were their enemies. For many generations, they battled. Few remembered that human beings were all related and created to live together as brothers and sisters.

No one spoke out for peace.

On a day when all harmony among created beings had broken, a great man came to their lands. He walked among the warriors and spoke of a Great Tree of Peace. Beneath it, all living beings lived in harmony. Its roots grew deep within the earth and spread through the land, uniting all places. The trunk of the great tree reached the above worlds and its branches spread out to shelter the earth. Among its leaves dwelt all the created beings.

"One of the chiefs was said to be so wicked he devoured his slain enemies. The Teacher of Peace found him and told him the story of the Great tree of Peace. His words created a vision of all beings living in peace within the branches of the tree.

The vision softened the chief's heart and restored harmony to his spirit. He traveled with the Teacher to other tribes, telling the story of the Great Tree and speaking of peace.

"When warring tribes learned the story, they united into one great nation. Since that day, they walked in harmony, strong in the teachings of The Great Tree of Peace. In unity, they prospered, rejoicing that war had ceased.

For as long as they remembered the Teachings of the Great Tree, no man would raise his weapons against another."

Twisted Hair lowered his eyes and stared into the fire, as if he had nothing more to say.

The people murmured in confusion. A warrior asked, "Why do you bring teachings of peace when our enemy stands at the gate? Are we to lay down our bows and give them our homeland?"

Twisted Hair said, "You are to teach your children that all human beings are the children of one creator. Hold the teachings of peace in your heart until a time when this is remembered, but it will not come in your day. The same wise teacher told of a great battle yet to come. This battle will not be among the tribes who united under the teachings of peace, for their union will hold. The war to come will be fought by two serpents."

The prophecy from the teachings from the northlands unfolded in the story Twisted Hair repeated.

"A great white snake will come from afar and lift his head above the land. A red snake will arise and go to meet him. His welcome will be mocked and the battle between the two serpents will shake the world for many generations. The red snake's strength is abundant, but in time it will fail while the white snake's power will increase. The day will come when the red snake will be defeated. He will lie as one dead, his spirit gone from him."

He paused to allow them time to absorb the strange things he told them. First, of the teachings of peace, then of war that spanned generations.

Kanagwa'ti said, "The white snake is here. He builds his houses along the river and hunts in our forests. Many have come already and there will be more."

The holy man beside him nodded. "The red snake lay as one dead. Are we the red snake who will die?"

Twisted Hair lowered his head sadly. "The red snake is our people. Like him, our children's children will be as dead people, for their place in the world will be taken away. They will wander in strange lands and be as hollow bowls, empty of spirit. Many will feel shame for their blood. They will forget the tongue of the ancestors and the wisdom it once spoke and become like the children of the white snake.

Do not despair, for a time will come when the children will look to the sky and see a sign. When they see it, they will know their day of exile is over and the spirit of our people will return. By this sign, they will know the time has come. Look to the eagle. When you see her fly her highest in the night and find no rest rest until she alights on the moon, then the red snake will rise, shake off his wounds, and stand proudly over his lands."

Twisted Hair wrapped his robe around his shoulders. Never before had he told this story and it drained his strength. He would leave it here and trust them to take it to the people. He heard them talk as the fires died down and the darkness deepened. The white snake, the red snake and the eagle became part of the knowledge they held to pass down to the children's children.

This much of his work was done. The prophecy of the day when the eagle flew her highest in the night and rested upon the moon, lay far in the future. Until then, the promise it held offered hope for dark times. One more thing he must tell them, a thing they would not like to hear.

"In generations yet to be, the children of the white snake will come to the red snake's children. They will ask them to share the teachings of The Great Tree of Peace and impart the sacred ways of the ancestors. Some will say, no, they have already taken too much. When they come to you, do not refuse to teach the children of the strangers. They are the people of the white door, the guardians of the fire. Through them, the sign of the Eagle will come."

No one spoke. They understood this too must be passed down through the children until it reached the generation that must heed it, the one that saw the night when the Eagle flew to the moon.

Far in the eastern sky, a faint light dawned. It was time. He beckoned the holy man and Kanagwa'ti. The young outsider would need the holy man's help with the burden he must bear.

They left the others by the fire, still speaking of the things the storyteller told them, sealing them in memory.

The holy man led them to the river bank. Under the light of the full moon, they purified with smoke, then seven times immersed under the chilling water. With prayers, smoke and water, they brought harmony to their spirits and made ready.

In a protective circle created by fresh cedar branches and the smoke of their purification, the storyteller opened his pack. When he freed the great blood-red crystal from its wrappings and laid it before them, it caught the glow of the first ray of the rising sun, devouring it and leaving a trace of darkness where it had been.

The holy man moved away from it but Kanagwa'ti stood fast. "This is the Ulunsu-ti?" he asked.

Twisted Hair nodded. "From among all our people, you are the Suye'ta, the chosen one. You have been selected by the Nunne'hi as the one who can use the Ulunsu-ti without selfish desires or foolish vengeance, to preserve our people. We will suffer greatly in times to come, but if you use this wisely, our people will not perish."

The Nunne'hi chose well. Kanagwa'ti accepted the gift of the Uku and surrendered to the duty and peril it brought to the guardian, but he must be prepared for the burden and the power it imbued on the one who held it.

For seven days, Twisted Hair, Kanagwa'ti and the holy man remained in a place apart. They took no food or drink and spent their time in prayer, seeking visions and dreams, and calling on the Above Beings to guide Kanagwa'ti. The young man would need their help for the work he must do.

On the seventh day, they purified once more with smoke and water. Twisted Hair surrendered the deerskin pouch and Kanagwa'ti took possession of the Ulunsu'ti and all the power and peril it held. It was in his keeping now, for good or ill.

The Nunne'hi women waited at Kanagwa'ti's lodge with a strong box, a gift fashioned by the hands of immortals. Kanagwa'ti placed the deerskin pouch and its fearful contents inside and buried it beneath his bed. A warrior, chosen by the holy man, stood guard at the door, just as the most trusted and strongest guarded the home of the old Uku, when the mother town remained in a world where warriors were needed.

The people of the village prepared a great feast and they broke their fast. While they celebrated his presence, Twisted Hair stole away unseen. The Nunne'hi women waited on the trail and they set out for home. The young outsider would stand or fall without further help from him, for he could stay no longer.

The years scarcely touched him in the mother town under the mountain, but they pressed down on him here. He followed the women through the unmarked forest, where the strangers didn't intrude.

He marveled at the beauty of the world outside the mountain of the Nunne'hi and wondered if he would see it again.

"You will return when you are needed," the Nunne'hi women said.

How many years would pass before he returned? He would not see Kanagwa'ti again. Perhaps his village would no longer stand when he came back. The Keetoowah sent the Ulunsu'ti in the hope that it would help a few of the people to survive, and his work was done.

He left nothing but his stories to comfort the Ani'yun Wiya while they suffered through the terrible changes destined for their homeland. The Ulunsu'ti must remain a secret known only to Kanagwa'ti and the holy man. The strangers, and even some of their own, craved power and would take it if they knew it lay hidden in a small village with only a few warriors for protection.

Tsi-s-qua had traveled long and become old. He came back to the mountain to heal from the hardships of his life. A boy named Sope took up the great totem staff and began his journey to a distant place where the people held great wisdom. The Nunne'hi sent him to bring the knowledge home for the Keetoowah to preserve.

A Twisted Hair would always walk among the Native people of the land to tell the story of their people. He drew solace in knowing that the work continued as it had for generations and drank in the sight of the mountains covered with smoke as the Nunne'hi women led him back to the hidden village.

Yes, many years would go by before he passed this way again and nothing would be the same when he returned.

On the path through the pines, memories weighed heavy on his soul. In the bend of the river where the mother town once stood, a rough cabin provided a lonely, isolated home. Cows grazed on the mound that still rose like a hillock beyond the cabin. No council house sat atop it, and no sacred fire burned.

The valley stretched ahead, and beyond it high on a mountainside, hidden among the trees, was the rock outcropping in the shape of the council house. He broke into a run for the rest of his journey home where the gentle woman waited for him.

With one last look at the world beyond the mother town under the mountain, he walked through the rock that stood between the world of the Nunne'hi and the world where he once lived.

The woman who waited for him was as young as when he first sat at her hearth. The Uku and the Ghigham looked no different than the day the Nunne'hi took them into the mountain. Corn, beans and squash grew in the gardens and the river sang as it wound through the valley. A ring of mountains rose beyond the town, casting purple shadows in the sunset. Chestnuts still weighted down the boundary tree and strawberries bloomed in the clearings. Nothing had changed within the ring of mountains, and the young had forgotten what used to exist beyond them.

Twisted Hair followed the woman into the lodge he had shared with her for more years than he could count. He was home.

Sope's Journey

 Sope rose early and went to stand for a moment beside his mother's grave, trying to remember her face. He recalled her voice and the last words she spoke to him. "This is your home now. You will be safe here." The town claimed him as their son.

The town looked smaller, and more worn than the last time he came with the Storyteller. Most towns did. The strangers spread through the land, claiming any part of it they desired, taking resources that once provided well for the people, and leaving many hungry.

He told his story of the future the Keetoowah saw, and left his people gathered in council to prepare for a way to survive. While they still talked, he stole away. He paused on the hilltop for a lingering gaze at the town that always welcomed him as one of their own, then departed before anyone could ask him to stay, or inquire where his travels might take him.

He feared there would be no town when he returned.

He couldn't tell them where his journey would lead. He didn't know. It would be longer than any he made with the storyteller. The song of the wisdom keepers said he must set his face toward the setting sun and go. With only that to guide him, he mounted his horse and leading the pony with his pack, departed the town that felt like home. He left the storyteller's white horse as a gift for the headman of the town.

He lodged that night in a village he visited many times with the storyteller. When they saw he carried the totem staff, they did not need to ask why. Sope was the new Twisted Hair and they honored him as they had the one who came before him. With deep sadness, they asked when Tsi-s-qua walked on to the above world. No one knew his age, but he had traveled among them before the oldest was born.

"He is not in the above world," Sope said. "I saw him pass through the stone and enter the mountain of the Nunne'hi. He waits there with the Keetoowah to hold the wisdom and sacred ways for the children's children. All who go in a sacred manner and listen, can hear the old ones speak."

They knew of the hidden mother town in the mountain of the Nunne'hi. Tsi-s-qua, the old storyteller told them about the Keetoowah and of the Twisted Hair who waited there, holding the wisdom for the time when it was gone from this world. Sope brought the story to their memory, of the immortals and the Keetoowah who welcomed the storyteller home.

"I will go to them when I'm old and tired, and they will take me into the mountain." Saying this gave him courage to tell the story of a future too dreadful to bear. With only one night for the telling he had no time for less weighty stories. The burden of the visions that still swam before his eyes, must be shared with the people before he could return to the mountain. By sunrise, he must leave them and continue his journey to the western lands.

He began by speaking of the spirits of the grand-mothers and grandfathers whose memories the land held, and the people cherished. "Where their bones lie, their flesh has become the land. Their breath is the air we breathe, and their voices speak in the wind. They nourish us in the fruits of the earth. This land is the gift of the Great One to our people. The Above Beings look down upon us here, and the Nunne'hi live among us. Never forsake them, for when they are forgotten, our people will be no more. When you are far from here, remember. When your children's children are ready, tell them to come home and reclaim their lands."

He sat in silence for a time to let his words seal in their hearts.

"You speak of this because you grieve for the story-teller," an elder said.

"I grieve the storyteller, but I will see Tsi-s-qua again when I'm old and tired. When I leave this world, he will be waiting for me. There is a greater sorrow that is to come, and I must tell you."

He saw dread steal over their faces as they prepared to hear the worst. He stood and held the great staff high before he began. He sang the song the Keetoowah gave him, warning of the invasion of the strangers and the fall of their people. When a cry arose, he silenced them and told his story.

The visions he witnessed came to life in his words. He spared them nothing, recounting the destruction of walled towns, death, hunger, defeat and the loss of the homeland and all the sacred places.

"Our trade routes will become their roads; our hunting grounds their plowed fields. Our rivers will run with their poison and our lodges fall into decay. The bones of our dead will be scattered, and sacred places defiled. Even now, it is so in many towns and villages. Without hope, the spirit of our people dies."

The young men resisted, as young men do. "No one can take our homeland," they shouted.

113

Sope said "In my journeys I have seen the great mound cities of the lowlands lying abandoned. The people who built them have disappeared. Their tongues are forgotten, and their stories are no longer told. Their lands are claimed by the strangers. Plows tear at the soil where the bones of the ancestors lie."

He raised his hands for silence when the young men talked of war. When they were quiet, he continued. "In the mountains formed by the wings of Grandfather Buzzard, the Ani'yun-Wiya still live, but the strangers build houses on our lands. They name us Cherokee, perhaps because they try to call us by the name of our home, Sha-cona-gee.

They are different from the ones who took so many lives in the lowlands and along the water, for they say they come in peace. They trade with our people and call us friend. In this is great danger. Our warriors have no need to fear our enemies, but the Keetoowah tell us a hard truth.

With kind words and promises, we will be broken."

With the warriors stirring the people to resist, he left them and went alone to the house where he would lodge for the night. There was nothing else he could say to them. His own loneliness and sorrow weighed too heavy on his heart. Exhausted, he fell asleep. He awoke before sunrise to find the chief and some of the elders waiting outside his door, bringing his pack filled with provisions for a long journey. He had thought to slip away unnoticed, to spare himself the pain of farewells he feared would be final.

They walked with him for a while, talking of the things he told them. Before parting, they asked him the same question he had asked the wisdom keepers. "Is there no word of hope you can give?"

He gave them the answer he had been given. "The spirit of our people is in Sha-cona-gee. Here, the wisdom of the ancestors will live. As long as a remnant of the Ani'yun-Wiya lives in these mountains, the sacred ways that give us our strength will not be forgotten. Teach this to your children. Tell them they must not forsake the homeland of the ancestors. Tell them to remember where they belong, and to return from distant places to reclaim this land. Here lies the hope of our people."

He left them and set out on a journey that took him far beyond the hills and into the low country. He entered villages where they waited for the return of Twisted Hair, remembering that the storyteller, Tsi-s-qua promised long ago he would come again. Some of them traveled to the mound in Sha-cona-gee to seek wisdom from the Keetoowah in the hidden village. The knowledge they brought home, sustained them through times of trouble.

Sope listened to their stories, and then told his own. He spoke of the hunger the strangers had for the land, not out of love or honor for the Earth as the home of the ancestor's spirits, but as a thing to possess. Then, he told of the journey he must make, and the reason he traveled west.

"The Great One has given visions to men of other tribes, showing the coming of strangers whom they called The Turtle People, and the changes these men would bring to the land. They have seen the future and speak of things to come in the days of the children's children. I go to learn their stories, for I must bring them back to the wisdom keepers in the mountain of the Nunne'hi. Knowledge can be held safely there, even when it is forgotten in the world beyond the sacred mountain. Though we are scattered and driven from our homes, there it will be remembered that we are all one in wisdom, spirit and blood. While this is held in memory, and a few of us remain on the land, we will live."

He told the wisest elders about the man dressed in black, reading from his book. *"I will lift up my eyes unto the hills."*

He left them wondering about the meaning of those words.

Sope repeated his story around many a fire, then departed each village at day break, leaving a subdued council to consider the bleak future that approached, and seek ways to prepare.

He left behind all that was familiar and rode out on a long hard journey. Beyond the high lands and valleys, to plateaus and beyond to flat dry lands where the sun beat down by day and cold deepened in the dark of night, he traveled.

Everywhere, the people remembered the Twisted Hair and the storyteller who followed him. They saw the great staff and welcomed Sope to lodge in their homes as they had generations of storytellers who preceded him. When he warned of the Turtle People, they told him of their fears. Even to these strange lands, the strangers found their way.

He traveled many days with a tribe that moved their whole town to the banks of a great river. There, they caught fish and dried them on racks in the sun. Among them was a man with red hair. The man took a wife from the tribe and she gave him children with skin almost as pale as his. Streaks of red ran through his son's hair. The red-haired man spoke the language of the tribe, and other tribes with whom he traded.

Sope stilled his suspicion and lodged with the red-haired man and his family. He listened to stories about the ways of the man's people in a faraway land across the great water. He learned to speak to the man in his own tongue, and the man listened and understood the stories of the people. When Sope told the story of the man in black and the words he spoke, the red-haired man showed him a book he carried with him in his travels. He opened it and read the words, *"I will lift up my eyes unto the hills."* The words that followed spoke of the creator of all things.

When the tribe left the river, Sope continued his journey toward the setting sun, remembering the red-haired man and the kindness he showed the people. *"With kind words and promises, we will be broken,"* the elders said. It troubled his spirit and helped him understand how calamity can come as a friend and corrupt from within. A good man who showed kindness and made them doubt their ways, was as dangerous as the men who came with weapons.

Years passed, and he still traveled across the land, over rivers, over bare jagged mountains that pierced the sky, past canyons that ran like wounds in the earth, through green forests and dry deserts. He spread his story among the people, always with the warning, *"With kind words and promises, we will be broken."*

He learned the stories and ways of the people he encountered, holding them in his heart, keeping every morsel to enrich the store of knowledge in the mother town under the mountain.

The journeys of Tsi-s-qua, the storyteller who came before him, took him to the Northlands. He learned from the people he met and took the knowledge back to the mountain. Sope's journeys took him to other people to learn new ways. Even before he reached his destination, he held a great store of knowledge to take home when he returned. In the dark times to come, it would be told around the fires of the Keetoowah, held safely under the mountain until a hoped-for future when the world outside would receive it again.

Sope aged in years and spirit on his journey. Weary and alone, he neared his destination. There on the mountain when they showed him his journey, the Nunne'hi placed a vision of the town before his eyes, showing him where he must go. He looked across the painted land and saw it in the distance. No vision could prepare him for what he saw. Houses the color of the earth, stacked one atop another against the backdrop of spires of stone and rocky bluffs, climbed above fields of corn.

He came closer and saw people high up on the walls and heard the voices of children at play. Women with baskets resting lightly on their heads, and men with bundles of wood, nimbly climbed ladders that leaned against the walls to reach upper lodges.

Smoke drifted up from cooking fires, carrying tempting aromas to the hungry traveler. He saw women grinding corn in the courtyards and making bread from the fresh ground meal. High up on the walls, men worked, adding another level of lodges to the dwelling. Unlike some of the towns devastated by the strangers, this town grew and thrived.

Though it looked different from any place he visited before, the town had a familiar feel. Tsi-s-qua told him about the mother town when it was still in the world. As he looked at the strange town, it brought images of the town under the mountain to his mind. He understood why they sent him here. This was a holy place for the keepers of wisdom, like the mother town, it housed knowledge that kept the sacred ways in the world.

He came nearer, thinking no one saw him, until a cry went up from the walls.

"The storyteller is here."

The people of the town ran to meet him, dancing and singing to welcome him with his stories. The weariness of the journey fell away, and he was at peace.

The story of Sope's journey preceded him, and the welcome he received was a balm to his spirit. They took him to the house of the chief where he lodged. Women brought the best of their stores to refresh him. Well fed, and clothed in fresh garments, he rested from his journey.

Drums called at the set of sun. The people gathered as they did in every town and village, waiting for his stories. They listened with rapt attention while he told of the sacred lodge in the mountains, and the wise ones who lived in the hidden village beneath it. He saw hope reflected in their eyes. The strangers had not touched their town, but they heard news of the destruction they brought to others. Whether because they were not so easy to find, or because the strangers saw no value in their arid homeland, they were spared the ruin Sope's people suffered.

Here, as in every village he visited, most of the people grew tired as the night wore on and drifted away to their beds. The few who remained by the fire were the ones who held the deepest wisdom and were eager to learn more.

When the moon rose high in the sky, an elder man beckoned Sope to follow him, then walked away from the circle. An old woman saw and did her part. She stood, drawing the attention of the gathering to her story. Sope was free to go. He fell into step with the elder behind other men who drifted discreetly away from the fire.

They wound among walls and courtyards until they reached a circle formed by a wall of stacked stones. Within the circle, a doorway led down into darkness. A hand on his shoulder guided him to his place and sat him down. He learned many new ways in his journeys and stored them in his heart to take back to Sha-cona-gee. This was another story he must take back to the wisdom keepers.

From the darkness beyond the closed circle, a light approached. A torch appeared through an opening. It revealed the face of a man who set it into a niche in the wall where it cast a dim glow around the underground circle. Someone lit cleansing herbs, and the fragrant smoke swirled among them. A drum sounded and the elder chanted prayers, then all fell into the deep silence.

When the elder spoke again, his voice echoed around the circle.

"From times of old, we have heard that three shakings of Earth would come, preceded by the coming of the Turtle People. When the strangers first came, we knew they were the Turtle People, for they walked like men but wore shells that turned away our arrows. When we heard they had arrived, we listened for the sounding of the first thunder of the shaking of the world."

He drew the scented smoke toward his face with an eagle wing and gathered his thoughts. A young man handed him a bowl and he drank from it and then spoke again.

"I will tell you of things to come, but first it is good to speak of the time of beginnings. In that long-ago time, all human beings lived together on an island in the middle of the great water, for all Earth was one land and all human beings were one people. There was no unhappiness for all pleasing things were there for them to enjoy.

For a long time, all the human beings were in harmony and lived in peace as brothers and sisters. War was not known for there was peace among all created beings. A day came when some of the people separated from the rest and went to live in the northern reaches of the island. Soon, another group moved apart to the South of the island. The ones who were left quarreled about who was at fault for their leaving, and soon they separated to the East and West of the island.

As generations passed, they stayed apart until the people of the four corners of the island changed and changed to fit the ways of the places they lived. When each looked at what they had become, they said, 'This is the way all human beings should be.' They looked at the others and despised them for their differences. All harmony among the human family was broken. For the first time since the Great One placed us in this world, brother shed the blood of brother. War had come into our world.

When the Great One saw how the human beings fought among their own families, his voice rolled like thunder through the land. The Island shook as he spoke of their pride and conceit, reminding them he created all the human beings as one family who would live together as brothers and sisters. The battle raged even as the land trembled.

For many days, thunder rolled, and the Island shook. The tumult didn't end until the people ceased fighting and sat down together to talk of peace. When they promised to walk the path of harmony, the thunder stilled, and the Island stopped shaking. The first shaking of the land ended, and human beings still lived.

For a long time, the human beings remembered the shaking of their land and walked in harmony. They talked of the thunder for many generations and remembered they were all children of the Great One. Their battles ceased, and they lived together in peace, as one family of brothers and sisters.

In the days of their children's children, the elders who remembered the first shaking left the world. The story of the thunder that shook the island was no longer told. Again, from the four corners of the great island, each one basked in pride for their difference, and contempt for the differences of others. Pride became anger, and blood was spilled. All harmony was broken.

Once again, the people from the four corners of the island gathered their weapons, each crying out against his brother.

Again, a deafening thunder rolled through the land as the Great One called out a warning. Mountains crumbled, rivers left their beds, and still the thunder shook the island. The people cried out in fear, but while brother spilled the blood of brother, the shaking did not cease.

After many seasons, they remembered the teachings of the elders and the sacred way of harmony and put aside their weapons. The thunder ended, and the second shaking of the island came to an end. For a time, the people walked in harmony and lived in peace as one family of human beings.

There were a few who could not enter harmony nor think of peace. The sickness of their anger spread, and before the generation of the second shaking passed from the world, they sent young men to make new weapons and prepare for a battle to come.

Now, it is said by the wise, that the Great One will warn once, and the Great One will warn twice, but the third time you stand alone.

This is how it happened on the Island of the first people. When the Great One called out to them for the third time, the thunder of his voice caused a shaking that tore the island apart. The lands of the four doors separated. The great Island was no more, and all the human beings fell into the sea.

The Great One showed mercy for his disobedient children. He spared their lives by lifting them from the water and placing them on the pieces of the great island that scattered to the four doors of the world. The people from the north of the island, he placed on a land that formed at the northern door of the earth. He named this the white door and gave its people two gifts. The first was a stone on which was written sacred words of wisdom and prophecies of things to come.

They took the stone and hid it beneath a mountain that rose high above their new home. Those who told the stories written on the stone forgot their importance, and time caused the meaning to fade from memory. As the generations passed, they forgot about the stone the ancestors secreted beneath the mountain.

The second gift to the people of the northern door was the guardianship of fire. He said, 'learn all it can teach and the good it can do. When you come together again with other human beings, live in peace as brothers and sisters and bring to them the teachings of the fire.'

The elder drank from the bowl and closed his eyes in thought. When he opened them again, he looked at Sope and said, "In speaking of the coming of the Turtle People, you speak of the spreading of the fire, for the nature of the fire is the nature of its guardian. The fire spreads and consumes, but as it spreads it brings together the family of human beings.

The Great One wants us to live together in peace as brothers and sisters. The people of the white door keep the guardianship given them by the Great One when they bring us together, but it will be many seasons before we learn to live in peace."

Sope nodded. "The strangers are the people of the white door. Their fire nature causes them to spread throughout the world. In this, they bring the human family together, but many are consumed."

When he knew Sope understood, the elder continued his story. "The people of the southern part of the Island now lived at the southern door of the earth. The Great One named this the black door and gave its people two gifts. The first gift was a stone on which was written sacred words of wisdom and prophecies of things to come.

The people of the black door took the stone and they too, buried it at the foot of a mountain, but some remember the writings to this day. The wisdom of the stone is sung in their songs and spoken in their stories. Then, the Great One gave the people of the southern door the guardianship of water. He commanded them to learn its teachings and power. 'When you come together again with all the human beings, come in peace to live as brothers and sisters and bring to them the teachings of the water,' he said.

The people of the southern door made their first home beside a great river. Its' rising and falling was the rhythm of their life. It marked the seasons, nourished the soil and taught them the wisdom of the water. They learned to live on the richness it brought to their new land.

The Great One placed the people from the eastern part of the island at the eastern door of the world. The Great One named it the yellow door and gave its people two gifts. The first was a stone on which was written sacred words of wisdom and prophesies of things to come. They did not bury it nor hide it away but took the stone to a place on a high mountain where they built a great lodge to house it. It is preserved till this day, and wise people still go there to learn of its wisdom.

"Then the Great One gave to the people of the yellow door the guardianship of the air. He said, 'Learn from it. Find what it teaches you, and when you come together with all the other human beings, come in peace to live as brothers and sisters, and bring the teachings of the air.' We have been told in visions and dreams that when we meet again with our brothers from the eastern door of the world, they will teach us to breath in the wisdom of the above beings.

Now, the people from western part of the island lived at the western door of the world. The Great One named it the red door and gave its people two gifts. The first was a sacred stone on which was written sacred words of wisdom and prophecies of things to come. The people of the red door took the stone and have kept it safe. The Great One placed it here, in our care. It is from this stone that we learned some of the prophecies of things that are to be.

"To us, the Great One gave the guardianship of the earth. He said we must learn from her, find her gifts, and when we come together with the other human beings, we must come in peace, to live as brothers and sisters, and bring to them the gifts of the earth.

When the strangers came to this land, the people of the red door met them bearing the gifts of the earth. We gave them the three sisters, corn, squash, and beans and taught them how to harvest the fruits of the earth. In this, and in honoring the earth and the unity of all her children, we have kept our guardianship.

Now the human beings have come together again, but not in peace. We have not heeded the warnings of the Great One. If we do not learn to live in peace and close the circle of the four doors, then will come the shakings of the earth."

Sope asked, "How will we know when the shaking of the earth begins?"

The elder approached the center of the circle and called for a torch. He uncovered a great stone that lay in a hollow of the floor and held the torch above it. The torch lit up symbols and pictures. Sope looked at it and could almost hear it speaking, so powerful were the images engraved on its surface.

"This is the stone on which is written words of wisdom and knowledge of what is to be," the elder said. "We are the keepers of the stone. It foretells many strange things that will come before the first shaking of the Earth. The coming of the Turtle People is written here, and the changes they bring to our people and to the world.

Here you can see through the eyes of one whose vision took him high above the land. When he looked down, he saw what seemed to be many little bugs traveling upon black ribbons across the land. In time, he saw that the little bug would leave the land and fly into the sky. Look for the sign of little bug, traveling the black ribbon across the land for it will bring people from the four directions to see each other face to face.

The time will come when the little bug takes to the sky. When you see this come to past, listen for the thunder. It will be the voice of the Great One, calling to our children's children to live in peace. If they do not close the circle of the four doors, uniting the human family, then the entire world will tremble.

This is the first shaking of the earth."

This new story inspired many questions for Sope. He added the elder's answers to the store of knowledge to take home to the wisdom keepers under the sacred mound at the end of his journey. The strange story of a little bug, and a black ribbon winding across the land, was beyond his understanding. He asked the elder to tell him more.

The elder traced the etchings on stone with his finger, pointing to a picture of things to come. "The little bug will increase, until more of them will travel the black ribbon than we can count. One day, others like the little bug will leave the earth and take to the sky."

What wonders the stone promised. Perhaps the Keetoowah would know the meaning of this new story and the etchings on the stone, but it was beyond Sope. He held it in his heart to add to the store of wisdom they preserved in the hidden town for the children yet unborn. They would need to know the signs that heralded the three shakings of the Earth, and how to prepare. The omen of the little bug must wait until then.

The elder continued with more that he must remember.

"If the people do not heed his warning, the thunder of The Great One's voice will roll across the land. Until harmony is restored, and human beings walk in peace, the world will shake. If the circle of the four doors is closed, the first shaking will end, and the human family will be blessed with gifts beyond our understanding. If human beings live in peace, we will receive all good things. If harmony is broken and we fall into ways of anger, the thunder will sound once more, and the second shaking will come. Tell the children's children to cry out for harmony among human beings when this day comes, for if they do not unite, they will cast the great gourd of ashes upon the land. Where it lands, all life will end like grass in a hot fire. Its poison will spread upon the world, causing vast numbers to sicken and die."

Visions of devastation swam before Sope's eyes, mingling with the images he saw atop the sacred mound.

"If the second shaking ends before the world breaks apart, you will see many strange things." The elder's voice echoed through the circle. "Human beings will build a house that shines in the sun as if it is made of mica. It will rise high above a great city in the East, higher than the tallest tree. In this house of Mica, the people will come from many lands to talk of peace. For peace to come, all the four sacred colors of the human family must be heard, and the circle of the four doors of the world must be closed.

In the time of our children's children, we must knock upon the door of the house of Mica and ask to be heard, for the people of the Red Door will be the last to speak. We must talk before all the people and tell of the wisdom found on the stone of knowledge. If we are heard, the circle of the four doors will close and human beings will have more time to learn peace. Tell the children that when they see the nations come to the House of Mica, they must knock the first time. If they are turned away, they must knock again. Four times, they must knock.

Watch for a time when people of many lands will work together to build a house and cast it into the sky. People from all the nations will rise up to live in it. Our children must knock the fourth time before this comes to past. If they are not admitted before human beings live in the house in the sky, the first thunder of the third shaking will be heard."

"What are the signs of the third shaking?" In the darkness, Sope's voice sounded small in his own ears.

The elder continued. "We do not understand the visions, for they show a strange world. We see men who have learned the secrets of life. They make new living things and say it is good. In the time of their children, it will cause great sorrow. They will bring forth living creatures that have neither mother nor father. Old sickness will come back, and new sickness will take many lives. They will use the secrets of the plan of life and change plants and animals until they no longer are part of the harmony of the earth and give no nurture. The three sisters, corn, beans and squash, will be barren. Their seeds will have no life in them. The Earth will grow tired and fail to bear fruit or grain. There will be hunger and thirst. Men will sit beside the river and weep because they have no water to drink.

A great web will spread around the world, and in its strands, all humanity will be united. If we have not learned to live in peace by then, the first thunder of the third shaking will sound."

Sope trembled at the thought of such a world. It was not a world he wanted to see. To hear it described brought fear to his heart, but this was a story the wisdom keepers must hear. He asked, "What is the sign of the third shaking?"

The elder answered, "When you have seen a house built by man and cast into the sky as a dwelling place for people of many lands, listen for the first thunder of the third shaking of the world. It will be heard in a great city with houses so tall they block out the sun. In the morning, the tall houses will stand. Before the day ends, there will be nothing left of them but smoke rising from ashes. When you see this, time will be short for it is the last warning. If we do not listen, the thunders will sound.

"It is said that a night will come when people will look into the sky and see the stars in the wrong place. Cold lands will be warm and warm lands will be cold. Water will cover dry places and rain will cease to fall in wet lands. In the end, the world will shatter. As in the days of the first people, the land will break apart and human beings will be separated to the four doors of the world again. The great web will be broken, and each man will stand alone."

"If our children's children heed the wisdom of the stone," Sope asked, "and close the circle of the four doors, what will our future be?"

"If human beings walk in harmony and learn to live in peace as one family, they will help the Earth bloom again. The four sacred colors will be one, and the children's children will be a golden people."

For a time, there was silence while they thought on these things, then the elder spoke to Sope.

"Take these words to the mother town under the mountain where they will never be forgotten. On your journey, speak of them to the elders among all the people who give you shelter, and tell them to remember. When it is time, we must speak of these things to all the people of this land, even the children of the ones who now bring great sorrow to us, for they too are a part of the balance and harmony. If we are to close the circle of the four doors, they must listen."

The elder gave Sope time to think of what he heard and store the words in his heart, then he asked him to speak of the visions he saw atop the stone council house on the mountain of the Nunne'hi. This would be added to the store of knowledge kept in the dark underground circle.

Sope's voice echoed in the silence as he told the story he came to tell. He told them of the sacred mountains covered with smoke, and of the sorrow of his people who lived there. When he spoke of the future he foresaw, of his people leaving their homelands never to return, they grieved with him. To lose the land blessed by the bones and breath of the ancestors, was more than any people could endure.

Through the night, they talked of things to come, and the words of wisdom written on the stone. Sope held the wisdom of the keepers of the stone in his heart, remembering each symbol on the stone and every word of the story. This is what the Keetoowah sent him to find.

When the elder asked him for the stories of his people, he spoke of the mysteries kept by the Keetoowah under the mountain. He told them of the mother town, the sacred fire that united all the clans in one spirit, and the green mountains where the mist rose like the smoke from a thousand pipes. With longing in his heart for the storyteller and home, he told them of the day the immortals took the mother town and the Keetoowah into the mountain to preserve it and the wisdom, until the people needed it most.

They spoke with awe of the mother town under the mountain, and the sacrifice the Keetoowah made, leaving the world they loved to live in the world of the Nunne'hi.

Sope said, "The Nunne'hi say your home will also be a place of safety where the memory of the ancestors will survive. The day will come when the eagle flies her highest in the night and does not rest until she lands on the moon. When you see this sign, welcome all who come to you and ask for stories and wisdom from the people of the red door. Hold this knowledge in your memory against that day. It is in your keeping until then."

Outside, the sun rose and traveled across the sky, but its rays did not touch the place of mystery where they gathered. Nothing entered that could distract them from their purpose. There in the light of a sacred fire, they shared the wisdom and knowledge held for generations and greater understanding dawned.

There is purpose in all things," the elder said. "The fire spreads and consumes, but those who bring it, open the way for uniting the human family and closing the circle of the four doors of the world. It is the Great One's will that all his children live together in peace, as one family of man. In this, let us find consolation."

They emerged from the circle in the hour when the moon lay just above the bowl of the earth and faint light tinged the eastern sky. The elders took Sope to a high mesa where they greeted the sun and purified with smoke. With half his duty done, he rested through the day and prepared for the journey back to the mountain, taking home the treasure of knowledge the Nunne'hi sent him to gather.

He ate well and slept soundly that night. When he arose, he found his pack filled with supplies and new clothing. His horse and the pack pony waited impatient to be on their way. The elder and village leaders walked with him to the trail beyond the town, telling him of towns along the way where he would find welcome and shelter.

When they parted, Sope reminded them of the story the storyteller brought back from the northlands. "Look to the sign of the eagle, for the time will come when our people will be as dead men walking upon the land. They will breathe and speak, but the spirit will be gone from them. For many years, they will forget who they are and the wisdom they hold, but when the eagle flies her highest in the night and does not land until she reaches the moon, our spirit will return to us and we will live once more."

Saying this, he turned his face toward the sunrise and began the long journey home.

Going Home

 Every town Sope came to on his return, welcomed him with questions about the mother town under the Nunne'hi's mountain. The legend spread, and even people who could never go there, listened to the story with rapt attention. A few felt a deep longing to take the journey and pleaded with him to tell them how to find the hidden town of holy people. He could see it in their eyes, they would soon set out find it.

The trail home stretched long ahead, and his heart yearned to return to the little village by the creek. Dark dreams held images of ruins and bones, but hope refused to die. He held onto the memory of old friends in the little town beside the creek and kept his face to the east. His travels took him to wander among the people of the western plains, hunting bison with tribes who told him stories of strangers who slew the great beast and left them to decay.

"Once they were thunder on the plains, mighty in their numbers, now the great herds are gone," a chief told him. "Now our people are hungry, and the buffalo die without honor and go to waste."

He watched the strangers build armed forts on grounds where the bones of the ancestors lay. Warriors fought bravely, but for every one of the strangers who died, ten came to take his place, and more of the people perished.

He was not a warrior and could not aid them in battle. Sope told his stories and lifted their spirits with

135

promises of a place under a mountain far away, where the wisdom keepers guarded the knowledge that gave strength to the Native People of the land. He gave them the new story from the west, of the great stone of knowledge and prophecy that waited in a sacred place where holy people kept it safe.

Late at night, when only the elders lingered by the fire, he spoke of things to come and bade them remember. He left them with the admonition, "look to the eagle. When she flies her highest in the night and comes to rest on the moon, then will our spirit be strong, and the sacred ways restored."

Years passed as he wandered through plains, mountains, deserts and valleys, always telling his stories and grieving with the people over changes that came to their lands. His greatest sorrow came from the young who lost their way and gave up hope. Even for some of the strongest, anger and despair broke all harmony in their spirit. The strangers claimed lands where once the people freely traveled. They built their homes and grazed strange beasts on sacred ground.

He found the wandering band with whom the red-haired man lived. Their camp was smaller, split in half to search for a new place to winter. Soldiers drove them away from the sheltered valley where generations of their people rested in the cold season. The son of the red-haired man remembered him, but his father no longer traveled with them. He went back to live with the strangers when troubles came.

Sope traveled hard the rest of the way, avoiding towns and leaving the trail when he saw the strangers. At night, he took shelter where he found it. Curled in a hollow tree or wrapped in his blanket under a ledge in the cliffs, he passed lonely nights and rose at dawn to be on his way.

When he stood beside the great river that marked the last boundary between him and journey's end, he looked across at the distant side and his yearning to go home grew stronger. He urged his horse and pony into the swift rapids, swollen by melting snow, but they shied away from the current. He turned upstream to find a safer crossing, regretting the days it added to his journey.

He came across a little village on the river banks where the people pleaded with him to stay, for the way was not safe for an old man who traveled alone. He welcomed the prospect of a few days of rest, and a chance to replenish his supplies, but impatience drove him on after the second night.

When the people of the village could not persuade him to stay, they offered to ferry him across the river in a boat made from a burned-out tree trunk. His horse and the pony pranced in the corral, ready to return to their life on the trail, but the boat would not hold them. He sadly left them behind and climbed into the boat.

He stopped for brief stays when he grew too weary to go on. His twisted hair brought requests for stories, and he put aside his need for rest and told them of the mother town under the mountain and the holy man who would come when his people needed him most.

He no longer warned them of the peril the strangers visited on the people. Few remained untouched by their greed. He turned a deaf ear to their pleas to stay and returned to the trail as soon as he rested and replenished his small store of supplies. Sha-cona-gee called him home, but first he must walk once more along the banks of the creek where the little village stood.

Green forests soothed him after his time in the desert. His spirits rose when he came to the creek that ran past the town he called home. He traveled its course, watching the sun sink lower behind him and the distant hills rising ahead. Tired and worn, he pressed on, delaying the need to rest until he reached his destination.

Anticipating one last respite among his people before he went to the mountain, he followed the creek toward home.

No one came to greet him when he drew near. With a sinking heart, he trudged on, dreading the worst. Around the last bend in the trail, he saw what he feared. Dreams that long troubled his sleep could no longer be denied. Only the scattered remnants of ruined houses and broken pottery shards, bore witness to the violent end that came to the town he called home. Fire left its mark on tree trunks and foundations. The stacked stone chimney that once rose from the council house still stood, a lone sentry rising above the ruins.

In the failing light, Sope wandered through the remains of the town, remembering old friends and wondering if they still lived. No one was there to tell him of their fate. He made his way to the place that honored an old and sacred memory he held in his heart for many years. Since Tsi-s-qua first brought him to the village where his mother lived her final days it called him home. The mound of stone he raised over her grave still stood, worn down and covered with moss. The oak tree shading it had grown tall in the years since he went away. It sheltered him that night as he slept beside his mother's grave.

Hunger woke him before dawn and his pack held no more food. He anticipated a feast on arrival in the town, but not even a grain of corn could be found. At first light of day, he fashioned a hooked spear from a poplar branch, and walked into the creek to spear a fish. On the bank, a child stood on a flat rock in the water. His hair fell long and dark across the copper skin of his bare back. Sope called to him, thinking one of the people of the town survived. When the boy turned, he saw his pale green eyes and remembered the son of the red-haired man, and many others in his travels who had the blood of the strangers.

Sope offered to share his fish with the boy. They sat together around a little fire while the fish roasted, the old storyteller and the child whose blood was of the Ani'yun Wiya but mixed with that of the strangers.

The boy asked many questions, then listened entranced, hungry for knowledge of his mother's people. His father did not allow her to speak of such things in the house he built for his Cherokee wife and son. Even the story of Grandfather Buzzard was new to him, and tales of the little people that all children once knew, were strange and wonderful to the boy.

When his father called him home, the boy pleaded with Sope for more stories, and promised to come tomorrow with his writing supplies.

Sope delayed his return to Sha-cona-gee and stayed with the boy. He left his stories with people across the land but found no one worthy to carry the great staff of the storyteller. The green-eyed boy cherished the legends in a way no one else had in all his travels. Could he be the one?

All through the spring and into summer, he camped beside the stream, telling stories to the boy and watching while he wrote them with pen and ink on the blank pages of a book his father gave him. "Pa likes it that I'm going to be a writer," he said.

For the first time, he saw the stories as written words. He no longer needed to trust the memories of people who struggled to survive and might not remain alive to keep the knowledge in the world outside the mountain. They lived in the marks the boy made in his book.

In mid-summer, the mountains drew him, and he had to go. He promised the boy he would return and told him the story of the great staff carried for generations of storytellers as they walked the land. He was yet too young to claim it, but he held it with reverence when Sope supported its weight it in his hands.

Sope left the boy beside the creek and turned his face toward the Smoky Mountains with a light heart. The mixed blood boy was not alone, for the blood of the Ani yun'Wiya still lived in a few who now made their homes in scattered farms along the creek. With his book filled with stories, and the memories of his ancestors awakened in his spirit, he would not forget.

Sope's steps were lighter and his heart at peace when the foothills came into view. Traveling in the high country and keeping to the cover of the forest slowed his journey, but he knew the strangers were more numerous now than his own people. He learned from bitter experience to keep to the woodlands and out of their sight.

On a cool autumn day, he stood atop a hill and looked down on a house built in the style of the homes of the strangers. It sat in a field surrounded by a low wooden fence. Two cows and a mule grazed in a pasture beyond. A man and woman stooped over rows of potatoes they unearthed and tossed into baskets. They dressed much like the strangers, but he saw long black braids hanging beneath the wide brimmed hat the man wore. A brightly colored kerchief covered the woman's hair. These were his people. He called out a greeting in the tongue of the Cherokee.

They stood and raised their arms in welcome.

He hurried down the hill to meet the couple who lived as the strangers lived. Leaving the baskets in the garden, they welcomed him into their home. Though their house and land were not like the homes of old, they were Ani'yun-Wiya in spirit. His heart rejoiced to be with his people again, to eat the food he craved and hear the language spoken in the way he remembered.

They told him about the changes that had come to their homeland. "The strangers take our houses for their own," the woman said. "At first, they shared our land, but soon more of them came. They forced us off the places they wanted to live and crowded us out of the land of our ancestors. Now, they build their towns, plant their crops, and graze cattle on the graves of our grandmothers and grandfathers."

Sope remembered his vision long ago as he sat atop the roof of the stone council house on the mountain. He saw broken hearted people leaving their homeland, knowing they would never return, and the strangers taking up residence in their houses. He wanted to think he would be gone from this world before it began, but it was already coming to pass. All joy left him at the thought of bearing witness to the anguish his people must endure.

Word traveled quickly that Sope had come back from the west. Many believed he would never return, and some doubted he existed. The Twisted Hair and the great staff of the storyteller had settled into the realm of myth. Tsi-s-qua and Sope lived in the legends they told the children and nothing more. Now that he stood before them, the great staff lifted high where all could see, new

141

hope came to the few who found their way to the farm-house and listened. They reverently touched the great staff, talking of the clans depicted, remembering the owl with four faces who watched over them all. A few had forgotten the clan of their family, and the rest helped them trace the line back to a grandmother who knew her clan.

Word of his journeys spread among all the Native people of the land. Perhaps he could offer wisdom that would turn aside the flood of strangers that threatened to force them from their homes.

He listened to their fears but could do nothing to comfort them. His words were more warning than solace when he spoke. "Your hope lies here in these hills. This is your strength. The spirits of our ancestors speak to us here and teach us to remember. Even when our people are scattered afar, they will look to this land for knowledge of their blood, and they will know, this is our home."

A woman said, "My grandmother tells a story of a lost mother town that once stood in the bend of a river. She says our people lived there 10,000 years, and kept a sacred fire burning to hold harmony among all our people. We told her it could not be, but she believes. She says we are the people of the one fire."

A man laughed. "It is a good story, but such a town could not be lost."

Sope silenced them all when he said, "I walked in the place where the mother town used to be and climbed the sacred mound where the fire once burned."

He told them of the Keetoowah, of the sacred fire and how it fed the fires of the seven clans, binding them as one people. He brought to their memory the wise Uku, the Ghigham, and the Twisted Hair who would come back to his people when they needed his wisdom most.

An old man said, "The storyteller came to us long ago with the story of how the Nunne'hi took the council house into the mountain. Many years passed before I traveled to see it, following the way he said we should go. On the mountain of the Nunne'hi, the stone protruded in the form of an old seven-sided council house. Shrubs and vines grew around it and hid its shape, but I climbed to the place I believed to be the roof. Two days I stayed before I heard the song, and when it came, I was afraid."

Sope understood his fear. He no longer sent people to the mountain. A few came back to their people with stories of the sacred ways that kept them strong, and names of revered ancestors. They remembered the place where the mother town stood and how long the people made it their home. They told of the warnings of dark days and encouraged them to be strong for the few who would survive. Others lost all hope and never returned to their homes.

Among those who gathered in the farm house, a few dressed and spoke much like the strangers. They worked among them and knew their ways. They spoke of things that greatly troubled Sope. One man said the strangers would take what they wanted, and no one could stop them. He advised trading with them for a place where the people could be left alone, to live in their own way far from the lands they desired.

Others greeted his words with anger, vowing to stand firm and hold the homeland, boasting of the warriors who were ready to fight to defend their homes the way warriors did from the beginning. They talked of courage, but fear haunted their every word.

They told Sope of the wise war chief, Junaluska. They said he fought beside a great white warrior who promised to defend the people from their enemies.

Junaluska believed some of the ways of the strangers were good, and the Cherokee would do well to learn from them. He warned that the Native People were hopelessly outnumbered. For every enemy the warriors killed, a hundred more came in his place.

A young man who wore the heavy shoes favored by the strangers, told of Sequoyah who learned to use the talking leaves. He showed them how to write Cherokee words and gave Sope a book with Sequoyah's writing. Cherokee could speak to each other with marks on paper and write the history and knowledge to preserve for the future.

He remembered the green-eyed boy beside the creek, who wrote the stories in his book.

A few saw no reason for fear and mistrust. They lived side by side with the strangers and prospered. Cherokee warriors fought beside them in battles, and some had married the strangers. Their children had the blood of both.

"The white men have become our brothers," they said.

Others remembered wise words spoken by a long ago elder. *"With kind words and promises, we will be broken."*

Sope listened, but memories of his vision atop the mound ran through his mind.

A man rose to speak. "Andrew Jackson is the new president. He will not betray us. Do you not remember that our Great War chief, Gul ka Laski, who is now called Junaluska, fought at his side in the battle of horse-shoe bend? When a Creek warrior would have slain the white soldier, Gul ka Laski shot the Creek and saved his life. The president is brother in battle to our warriors and owes his life to one of our own chiefs. He will see that our lands are protected."

Their words held the ring of truth. Surely, the man who owed his life to Junaluska could be trusted. He acknowledged his debt, admitting the Americans would have lost that battle without the help of Gul ka Laski and his Cherokee warriors. Had he not made a vow of friendship and promised to reward them?

The strangers outnumbered the Cherokee people in their own homeland. That could not be denied. More came every year, encroaching on well-tended farms and rich woodlands where the people lived. The Cherokee lands were the best to be had, and those who begrudged it would stop at nothing to take it.

The vision he saw on the roof of the council house rock swam before his eyes. He felt its approach draw ever near. With dawning awareness, he understood, he must suffer with his people in their hardest hour and bring this final story back to the mother town under the mountain. Unable to spare them, he could only walk among them and observe.

It unfolded as he watched. He remembered the words of a warrior where the desert gave way to the mountains, "They dig at mother earth to find something that is without meaning to us, yet they will kill us all to take the land where they find it."

When he heard rumors of gold in the North Georgia Mountains, he knew it sealed the doom of the Cherokee way of life. If the land held nothing more than farms and woodlands, greed would not drive so many to them. With a lust for gold even more powerful than the hunger for land, the strangers poured in.

Subterfuge and deception were powerful tools. He watched as unscrupulous men gained title to the sacred homeland, and the people could do nothing.

Even when uniformed soldiers came with orders that all the Native people must leave their homeland, the Cherokee held on to hope. Sope traveled to the council where the wisest leaders planned a delegation to send to Washington to speak with the man who called himself their brother. Junaluska and Chief Drowning Bear departed with confidence, knowing no honorable man would break his word to a brother in battle. Jackson owed his life to Junaluska, and Chief Drowning Bear lost his son in the battle of Horseshoe Bend. The president would honor their sacrifice and rescind his orders that robbed them of their home.

The people planted fields and tended live stock. They mended fences and cared for their houses, unable to accept they might lose everything.

All hope dissolved into desolation when Chief Drowning Bear and Junaluska returned, crushed and disheartened. In disbelief and with broken hearts, the people heard the news. Jackson turned his back on the Cherokee. All promises broken, all pledges denied, and treaties ignored, the president they trusted betrayed them.

Chief Drowning Bear said, "We fought his battles, we lost warriors and suffered for his cause, but now that he has no need of us, he turns us away. 'What have I to do with these people,' he said when we asked to speak to him. We waited outside his door, and he would not let us in."

Sope saw desolation become the companion of all his people. Their despair engulfed him, but he could not turn aside. Everything that occurred must be remembered and added to the story against the day when the descendants might forget.

The next part of the story began with shouts of the people and the noise of horses. Sope stood aside and witnessed the first moments of his final vision on the stone roof of the council house. A column of soldiers rode onto Cherokee land. He looked on the face of the man who led them and remembered looking at it through the eyes of spirit, long ago, before the man was born. Now, Sope saw him in flesh and blood, the man who troubled his dreams on dark nights under the stars. He listened and learned his name. General Winfield Scott.

The solders saluted and did his bidding, setting out across the land, rounding up the Native People at the point of rifles, showing no mercy for man, woman or child.

Sope listened to the stories of people the soldiers brought to the stockades, herded inside like cattle and imprisoned. Even the dead were not respected, they said. They told of soldiers who came to a cabin where a mother and father prepared their dead child for burial. The mother wept when she told how they forced her to leave the body of her little girl behind, unburied.

A woman's family told how soldiers dragged her from her bed and ordered her to walk, though she was too weak and sick. She died on the road. The soldiers forced her children to leave her there on the ground and walk away.

The stockades grew crowded as the summer wore on. In every mountain, valley and cove, the soldiers hunted down Cherokee people and drove them off to stockades built to hold them. "What will they do with us," the people asked.

No one answered, but a rumor whispered through crowded stockades. When Winfield Scott captured the last of their people, strangers would claim their homes. A forced march westward lay ahead for the Cherokee.

The warrior spirit remained strong in the people who loved the land. Battered, but unbroken, some fled to the mountains. Families left their homes and took shelter in caves or makeshift dwellings, living off the land.

The soldiers searched, but the people knew the wild places of the Smoky Mountains, too rugged for outsiders to follow.

In the stockades, the captured Cherokee looked to the hills and found hope. If a few could remain in the homeland and continue to fight for the rights of the Cherokee, perhaps they could reclaim their ancestral home.

They walked away with the soldiers, watching as squatters moved into their houses and harvested their crops. They had no right to object when the strangers slaughtered livestock and took their horses for the army.

The vision that haunted Sope's sleep since he stood atop the mound and saw the future unfold, took shape before his eyes. He could do nothing but watch.

He heard the soldiers speak of a man General Scott ordered them to find. They called him Tsali, and said he killed one of the soldiers. Sope listened and learned there was more to Tsali's story. The soldiers came for his family, took away their weapons and forced them from their home. Unarmed and outnumbered, they went peacefully, but when a soldier dishonored his wife, Tsali, with his brothers and sons sprang to her defense.

The soldier died.

Tsali and his family fled into the hills.

"We can't let an Indian get away with killing a white man," a soldier said. "That would give the rest of them ideas."

The soldiers ranged the hills on a futile pursuit of the renegades. Tsali knew the mountains of his homeland far better than they. Generations of his people lived and died in the mountains and knew places strangers would never find.

General Scott came up with a cruel but effective solution. He announced to all who could hear that if Tsali and his family surrendered, all the other Cherokees hiding in the hills would be left alone. If not, Scott's soldiers would hunt down and kill the last man, woman and child until not a single Cherokee remained in their ancestral home.

It seemed to please him to watch all hope die and despair settle over the people.

Chief Drowning Bear sent his adopted son, to find Tsali and give him Scott's message. The chief's son was a white man, Will Thomas, known to the Cherokee as Will Usdi. Chief Drowning Bear gave him that name when he adopted the white soldier to take the place of his son who died in the battle of Horseshoe Bend. It meant Little Will in the Cherokee tongue, for he was small in stature.

Will Thomas proved to be a faithful friend to his adopted people, and one of the few white people who could still be trusted in those troubled times. He climbed into the hills with the burden of Winfield Scott's demand. Not only must Tsali return, but his sons and brothers. To surrender meant the white man's firing squad, but if he stayed safely in hiding, it meant death for many more of his people. With no one to remain behind and fight for the homeland, they gave up all hope of re-claiming it.

Sope observed a story of courage and sacrifice unfold. Tsali and his family deserted the safety of the hills and came to face General Scott's justice, knowing it meant certain death.

Did he know his memory would live to inspire generations of his people?

Condemned, Tsali, his brothers, and sons stood straight and proud, walking to meet their death.

When they allowed one last request, Tsali asked that Cherokee marksmen serve as executioners. He trusted them to render a quick and merciful death to his sons.

His request granted, the marksmen took their places, raised their rifles, waiting for the order to fire.

Before the order came, A man in a long black coat ran before the rifles, pleading for mercy.

The memory of his vision swam before Sope's eyes. The man in black. The dread instilled by the vision flooded over him as he listened to the man's impassioned plea.

"Who is he?" he asked a woman beside him.

"A good man," she said. "He and his wife stood by the Cherokee in our troubles."

While her husband pled Tsali's case, the woman dashed in front of the marksmen. Clutching Tsali's youngest son to her breast, she ran until she was out of sight.

The general allowed this one small mercy and let her go. Even he couldn't tear a little boy from a woman's arms and let him die.

Her husband stayed to offer comfort to those who would die, reading from his book that promised they would live again in the above world.

Sope turned his head away when the shots fired. The man in the black coat said prayers for the dead, then left to find his wife and the Cherokee child.

Tsali's son would be safe with them.

The soldiers ignored Sope. He was an old man who never spoke, dressed in the garb of another time, with no family or friends. A young soldier found him standing alone, watching as they took the dead from the field. The soldier spoke to him in the Cherokee tongue. "You must come with me, grandfather." Sope heard a hint of regret in his voice.

Sope took his place with the people, sharing the same fate they faced, keeping their story. The soldier led him to the stockade and put him behind the wall with his people. He sat on the packed soil just inside the gate with no shelter from sun or rain.

The young soldier gave him a blanket and a drink of water from his canteen. A child came and leaned against the soldier's leg.

"He is kind to us," she said to Sope.

If there was kindness among the soldiers, Sope needed to hear his story. He spoke to the young man in his language, asking how he came to be among Winfield Scott's men. The red-haired man on the plains taught him enough to communicate with the strangers.

"So, you can speak," The soldier said. He went on to tell Sope the story of how he became a friend to the Cherokee. "My name is John Burnett. I went hunting one day when I was just a youngster. I heard a noise from the bushes and went in hope of easy game. I found a Cherokee boy hiding in a thicket, the prey of white men who chased him for sport. He was nearly dead from thirst and loss of blood and would have died if not for the good fortune that brought me his way. I gave him

151

water, cleaned his wounds, and looked after him until he gained the strength to travel. I helped him get home, and his family took me in. I learned to speak the language from them. I stayed until I joined the American Army and went away. When General Scott needed Cherokee speakers, I volunteered. Maybe I can make the way easier for the people. Speaking the language makes me an asset to the army, and I do my best to help when I can."

Sope observed that Private Burnett as well as a few of the other soldiers did what they could to ease the suffering of the Cherokee. In the high heat of summer, soldiers brought fresh water to thirsty people and helped them rig makeshift shelters in the open stockade. Their kindness kept some of the weakest alive.

The season passed and cold came early that year. A chill October morning dawned when no kindness could ease the anguish of the Cherokee. Drizzling rain slanted in a freezing wind, cutting through thin clothing. A line of wagons stood ready to roll, loaded with the weak and old. A few of the more fortunate had buggies or carriages and some rode horse back. Most would walk the long trail west.

From the back of an aging horse, Sope watched as the vision that came to him atop the mound unfolded. Just as he saw it long ago, soldiers lined up with their rifles. He watched the man in a long black coat climb on a loaded supply wagon where he could be seen and heard by the people. He bowed his head and prayed, then lifted his eyes to the encircling mountains and in a loud voice read words from his holy book.

"I will lift up mine eyes unto the hills from whence cometh my help."

When the people lifted up their eyes to the hills, did the man in a black coat know they drew on the only hope left to them? There, a few remained undiscovered, hiding in caves and forests until the day when they could come down and reclaim the land of their ancestors.

The soldiers shouted marching orders.

In sadness beyond bearing they said farewell to the beloved land they would not see again and turned their faces to the west. Men who thought of the land only as a possession, could not imagine the depth of sorrow its loss brought to people for whom it was a sacred homeland. Here, the ancestors slept. Memories stretched back through generations of Ani'yun-Wiya. Here the air they breathed was the breath of those gone before and the land itself was their flesh and bones, returned to the earth.

Sope took one last look in the direction of the sacred mound, and on to the mountain of the Nunne'hi rising beyond into the mist. He longed with all his heart to leave the sorrow of the outside world and join his people who waited for him there, but he had more stories to learn and take home to the wisdom keepers.

He drew a tattered blanket around him, turned his face to the west and fell in behind the wagons, watching and remembering.

The cold of winter set in early and added its icy chill to their misery. Wind-driven sleet and snow took their toll. Many had no blankets. Most had only the ragged clothes they wore when the soldiers drove them from their homes. At night, they slept in the wagons or on the cold ground. Every daybreak found more people dead from exposure.

Chief Ross's wife gave up her only blanket to a sick child. The good woman, who did her best to care for the sick, died during the night. They buried her in a shallow grave beside a trail marked by many of their dead. There

153

had no coffin for her body, not even a blanket to wrap her, for the living needed warmth more than she. What she gave freely in life, she would not have wanted in death.

Through the coldest months of the winter, they walked the Trail of Tears. In forests, fields, and on rocky plains, they left four thousand shallow graves to mark their passage. At each one, they vowed to come back and return the bones to lie with the ancestors in the homeland.

Junaluska could have stayed in his farm on Deep Creek, the one small mercy granted him for his service to the American Army. The old war chief declined, and chose to walk the trail west, casting his lot with his people. Perhaps his leadership would make the way a little easier.

Was it guilt that made President Andrew Jackson offer to let him keep his home? He vowed kinship with the Cherokee, then signed the act that robbed them of their homeland. He accepted their help and made promises he never intended to keep. If he had any honor in his heart, the burden of his deeds would torment him the rest of his days.

Junaluska suffered hardship along with the rest on the trail. He carried tired children when they faltered and gave his meager goods when someone needed them more.

The women gathered tattered clothing and fashioned shirts from cloth torn to ribbons. Men wore their ribbon shirts with pride, celebrating the ingenuity of their wives.

They reached the wild, rocky land allotted them. Their people who went before to prepare, welcomed them helped them settle in.

Sope pitched in to help, becoming part of an efficient work force, building shelters and breaking ground to prepare for the planting time. His heart swelled with pride as he watched them put aside grief to make a home where they could provide for the children.

The rocky, untamed land demanded long days of backbreaking labor to prepare, but the fertile soil held promise.

With crops germinating in the ground, and every family housed, spirits lifted. Abundant wild game flourished in forests, and fish swam in clear rivers and streams. A new community flourished, but it wasn't home. At night, when the work was done, and all was still, talked turned to memories of Sha-cona-gee.

Junaluska talked of the people who remained to reclaim the land. He felt the call of his duty to keep the place of his ancestors for the Cherokee.

When they pleaded with him to stay, worried about the long journey for a man who had lived a long, hard life, he said, "I can do no more here. Those who remained behind in the hills hold our place in Sha-cona-gee where the spirit of our people survives. I must go to them and do my part for our homeland."

"I will lift up my eyes unto the hills," Sope said.

A little band formed to travel home with the beloved Junaluska. Sope joined them, watching and remembering. When they came across one of the graves they left on the trail, they gathered stones to mark them. It was a small way to honor the dead who died so far from home.

"Someday," they promised at every graveside, "We will bring your bones home to rest with the ancestors."

First sight of the mountains of home, brought tears of joy. Junaluska grieved the loss of his farm on Deep Creek. It now belonged to strangers. They traveled on

155

across the mountain to an isolated Cherokee community on Snowbird Creek, where Junaluska made his new home.

The impoverished people accumulated deeds to land by using all they could earn to purchase acreage they once owned. As a white man, Drowning Bear's adopted son Will Thomas could do something no Indian could do. He could buy land and hold title in his name.

Sope found his place in the community, just an old man who remembered the stories and told the people of their past.

The young had no time to listen. Providing for families and procuring claim to their homes, occupied their waking hours. Every acre they purchased brought them closer to restoring a community where the descendants of the Ani'yun Wiya could hold a place in the land of the ancestors.

What more did he need to see before the Nunne'hi called him home? He waited and listened, always telling the stories of the people to the children. In them lay the hope for the future, and through them, the story of the heroes would live.

He told them of Tsali and his brothers and sons, and Junaluska, the great man who led the people to the West and then came home to encourage those who stayed behind.

When he heard the children speak in anger, he reminded them of friends among the outsiders who showed kindness to the Cherokee. Will Thomas, a faithful son to Drowning Bear, helped his adopted people reclaim their homes. The man in the long black coat offered more comfort and hope than he knew, and his wife saved Tsali's son from the firing squad. And there were the soldiers who showed compassion in their darkest times.

Sope told his stories around evening fires when the people gathered, sealing in their hearts the memory of their ancestors, the sacred ways, and the heroes of renown. In the days when the people lost their spirit, and walked as dead men on the earth, great deeds such as theirs would serve to lift heavy hearts.

The heroes of Sope's stories grew old and left the world. Junaluska's bones rested on a hilltop near a town of the white people. The great chief had seen the realization of his hope to regain a home for the Cherokee in the ancestral lands, and helped it be declared a reservation that could not be taken from them again. The children who remembered, grew up and told Sope's stories to their children.

Sope's work was done.

The trail called once more to the old man. The memory of a green-eyed boy beside the creek that ran past his mother's grave, tugged at his mind.

Secure in the knowledge that the rest of the story of the Eastern Band of Cherokee was in good hands, he stole away unnoticed. He climbed the hill to Junaluska's grave and placed seven small stones there to honor the hero who sacrificed so much for his people.

Filling his eyes and heart with the beauty of the greening mountains, he prayed for his people, then took up the totem staff and set out toward the place he went when he craved the feel of home.

Moss and vines covered the scattered mound of stone that marked his mother's grave. The ancient oak tree still sheltered it and gave him shade while he waited for the call to the mountain.

On a morning when Sope roasted a freshly caught trout on a hot stone in his fire, an old man waded into the creek, holding the hand of a little boy. He sat across the fire from Sope and smiled, his green eyes set deep in his wrinkled face. "I'm glad you came back, grandfather," he said.

The little boy said, "Grandpa said you would tell me stories when you came,"

Sope showed him the great staff and taught him the meaning of the clan symbols. The boy looked up at the owl with four faces and said, "He sees in all directions and knows all things."

In the days that followed, Sope told the boy stories, and taught him to discern secrets hidden in their core for the wise ones to discover. He described the journey he made to the west and what he learned about the great stone and prophecies of things to come. He brought to life the lost mother town in the bend of the river, and the mound where the council house sat, and the sacred fire burned.

The boy absorbed every morsel and craved more. In all his travels, Sope looked for someone to take his place, and none proved worthy. This young boy, who cherished the ways of his grandmother's people, would bring a new element to their story.

The years weighed heavy on Sope. Faint voices called in the wind and he longed to turn his steps to the mountain. How could he go when there was no storyteller to leave behind? In days to come, his people would need the Twisted Hair and the boy was not ready to take up the great staff and travel the land.

The voices in the wind called louder and he could no longer resist the longing to go home.

He told the boy and his grandfather he must go. This time, he would not return.

"We knew this day would come," the grandfather said. "My grandson is not old enough yet, but I will help him prepare. Until he is ready to go to the people, we will keep your stories in a book, so they will always be remembered."

The boy asked to hold the storyteller's staff. He stood, and Sope placed it in his hand, resting it on the earth to support it. The boy read the secrets of the staff with understanding of the stories it told. He revealed the stories of every creature, and what they meant to the clans they represented. He knew the owl with four faces circling, the head of the staff, spoke of the spirit of the Great One who ever watched over his children. He saw them in all the directions they might wander.

With peace in his heart, Sope told him one last story. He gave him the way to the lost mother town, forgotten by most since the Trail of Tears, and told him how to find the Mountain of the Nunne'hi and listen to the wise Keetoowah within.

The grandfather carried the staff when they waded across the creek to the house on the other side. Sope watched until they were out of sight, then took one precious white stone from his pack. Taken from the river that ran beside the mother town, carried to the west, and back to the people and on to the Trail of Tears, he carried the stone that connected him to Tsi-s-qua, Twisted Hair, and the sacred mountain. He didn't need it any more.

He placed it on his mother's grave and departed the only place he ever called home.

Of Things to Come

 It was a small gathering that night around the fire. Most of the people who came to dance in the sacred circle, had gone home or wandered in the field beyond the dancers. The few who lingered at the fire, talked about the old times when their people were the only ones who lived in the Smoky Mountains they called Sha-cona-gee. They repeated ancient stories of sacred beings whom the elders claimed lived among them. The immortal Nunne'hi, the tiny Yunwi Tsunsdi, the little white deer they called Awi Usdi, and all the others who were seldom, if ever, seen anymore. Some said they no longer existed. Many believed they never had, except in stories told by the grandparents.

The world had changed since the days when their ancestors were called Ani'yun Wiya. Some of the changes made them fear for the land. The waters flowed in the rivers and creeks as it always had, but they couldn't drink it. Where fish once filled the streams, few were seen. The smoky mist that shrouded the sacred mountains, now poisoned the trees in places and caused sickness for children and elders. The great chestnut trees no longer grew. If ever they needed the wisdom of the sacred beings from the old stories, it was now.

A young woman spoke up. She would soon leave the Smoky Mountains and go to live far away with her new husband. She spoke to honor the memory of her grandmother whose bones rested on the hillside that rose beyond the field. The few around the fire settled down to listen, but the voice of a new arrival broke the silence.

161

The Twisted Hair felt their welcome when he stepped into the circle. He was a stranger in their midst, but they recognized him as one of their own.

"Osiyo," he greeted them in the ancient language of their people

They made room for him at the fire. A younger man stood and invited him to sit on the bale of hay he used as a seat.

"Wado," Twisted Hair thanked him. He stretched out his hands to warm them by the fire. An early spring chill touched the mountain air.

The people watched him without a word, waiting for him to tell them who he was and where he came from. He saw how they marveled at the intricate beading and quill work in his deerskin leggings and tunic. His moccasins were fine enough to be the envy of the best dressed dancer, but they bore the marks of wear.

One of the young dancers stared in open admiration at the stranger's garb. The boy wore ceremonial regalia and would have been the pride of his clan in days past.

Twisted Hair watched the clumps of people in the field beyond the fireside, waiting for them to notice that a newcomer had arrived. When they saw him, their curiosity drew them back to the circle.

His sharp hearing picked up soft voices. "You can see he's Cherokee, a full blood. His features, the color of his skin, his bearing. But who is this stranger who comes from nowhere. And what's with the hair-do?"

He smiled in the darkness and waited.

A wiry, grey haired woman squatted on the ground at his feet and peered into his face. Her black eyes twinkled with the wisdom of many years. She spoke in English accented with the essence of the mountains.

"I've told the young'uns stories about a wandering holy man who remembers for the people. They say the holy man was the only one who could wear the twisted hair. The way my grandmothers told me, was that he would come to us when we most needed him, when there was something important we needed to know. The young'uns didn't believe me. But nobody here has ever seen a man like you. Nobody has seen the Twisted Hair."

Twisted Hair sat up tall and let them look at his hair, hanging long past his waist and resting against his hips. Twisted into thick ropes and held at the crown with beaded thongs and black as night, only a few streaks of silver showed the passage of time.

"It's the mark of the holy man of old. It fits the stories the elders told of the holy man who would return when we most needed his wisdom," the old woman insisted.

"It's just a story," one man said. "We're not supposed to take it literally."

A doubting man said, "Grandmother, I've heard the story, but this couldn't be the same man. This man is too young. He could not be the holy man returned."

In the land of the Nunne'hi, lines did not touch his face, and his body remained straight and strong. Twisted Hair expected the people in the circle to question the old woman's story He reached into the deerskin pouch at his side and withdrew something. The growing crowd strained to see what he held. It looked like an ordinary newspaper. He opened it and sat silently reading it by the firelight.

The man nearest him asked a question. "Are you from the Cherokee Nation in the west come for the pow-wow?"

Twisted Hair said, "I live in a town in the mountain, over there." He gave a vague wave toward the Mountain of the Nunne'hi.

He turned to the young woman whose story he had interrupted. "I have been to your home on the Cheoah, *uweji agehya?"* He used an old term meaning my daughter.

She nodded. "My family has lived on the Cheoah in Graham County for generations, but we have not seen you there."

This would be a puzzle to her. In such a small community, no Cherokee went unnoticed. Twisted Hair offered no explanation. He asked her forgiveness for the interruption then added, "I would be honored if you would allow me to listen while you speak of your grandmother."

The young woman stammered at first, a little intimidated by the stranger, but the story she told was a gift from her grandmother and she told it in her memory.

"I live in a little house beside the Cheoah River. Soon I will go away to live with my husband in a big city where I can't hear the River's song. Only my grandmother understood how this would sadden me. Before she walked over to the other world, she gave me a story of another girl who loved the river as much as I do. This is the way my grandmother told it to me.

"Long time ago in a village beside the river, a baby girl was born on the coldest, darkest night of the coldest, darkest winter. The first thing the little baby heard was the wind howling outside. The cold found her, even wrapped in a warm blanket and held close by her mother.

Darkness filled the lodge she entered, and it seemed to the baby girl that the whole world was dark and cold. She cried in fear. Outside, River heard her cry. He sorrowed for her, knowing she had never seen the sun and didn't know of summer.

River sang to the baby girl. His song promised sunshine, flowers and bright colored birds who would sing their songs for her. He sang of how warm she would feel in the spring and how soft breezes would take the place of the howling wind.

His song eased her fear and she understood that the winter would go away, and warmth would come. The smile she sent River warmed him and cracked the heavy ice that rode his back.

Through the winter, River sang to the baby girl every day. Soon she could sing back to him, in her own way, and her smiles and laughter warmed him.

At last, Cold Maker went away, and Sun warmed the village. The mother laid her baby on the soft grass of River's bank, and the baby heard his song. When her mother looked away, the baby crawled as fast as she could to the very edge of the water.

In her joy at seeing the one who sang away her fear, she reached out to touch him and fell into the rushing water.

Her mother cried out for help. Her father and the other people of the village hurried to rescue her, but she was nowhere to be seen.

Young men took canoes out to search but could not find her.

When they had given up hope and sat weeping beside the water, a spray from the rapids lifted the child and laid her upon the shore.

Her people understood. They need not fear the river. The baby girl was safe in his care.

When she grew older, her father cut a tree and made a canoe just big enough for a little girl. In it, she traveled with River and he told her stories of all his journeys. She longed to go with him to the place where he joined the big water, past the forest and green fields, to see all the things he told her about in his songs. He said no. She must stay close to her people.

Her people called her River Girl for that is where she could always be found, in her little canoe on the river. When she was a young woman, many young men came to ask her mother to allow them to seek her favor.

The mother said, 'She will have no husband but River.'

A time came when the rains did not fall. Game was scarce in the forest and the fields yielded little. In the village beside the river, the people worked hard to store enough to last for the coming winter. Cold Maker came early and stayed long.

The River Girl's people had enemies who did not provide for their own but sent warriors to take that which others prepared. They attacked her village before the sun rose, bursting from the forest without warning to steal the grain and meat they stored.

The people fought bravely. When River Girl's father fell, she took up his bow and fought in his place. When her people saw her courage, it inspired them to fight. They defeated and saved the winter provisions.

Among the dead warriors, lay the river girl and her father.

Now, there is a place where only fallen warriors can go. The spirit ponies come to gather the warrior spirits and take them there. River Girl's father and the other dead mounted the ponies. They searched for her, for her courage won her a place among warriors in the above world. They looked for her through the village and into the forest. Her father went to the house of her mother, but her spirit wasn't there.

With nowhere else to look, her father went to the river. He heard her voice. It was faint, almost drowned by the deeper voice of River, but he heard it clear.

River Girl sang River's song with him. Her spirit travels with him on his journey to the places in his song.

If you stand silently beside the river and call to her, you can still hear her voice. She will sing with him as long as River runs his course."

The young woman sat beside her mother. Her mother embraced her and brushed tears from her cheeks. It is hard to send a child into the world. In the old days, a husband would come to live with the mother's clan, but times changed.

Twisted Hair stood and thanked the girl for her story. It was one he had not heard before.

The gathering turned their attention to him when he spoke. "I too am a storyteller but most of my stories are far older than the one your grandmother gave you. Some you still know, and others you have forgotten."

He lifted his voice until even those still strolling about in the field beyond the circle heard. "I have come tonight to bring a story that is even now unfolding."

From the darkness around the ceremonial grounds, people hurried back to listen. The elder woman whispered, *"The Twisted Hair."* The words carried as if shouted into the silence. The stranger stood tall, waiting for the right time.

In the expectant silence, the old woman rose to her feet. Her eyes filled with tears and she hesitated to speak, but the stranger nodded in her direction. She spoke haltingly at first, and then in awed tones raised her voice to tell an almost forgotten story. In her words, the lost mother town lived again. She brought to memory the elders who held the wisdom of the people, of the town that sat in the bend of a river with the sacred mound rising above it. She talked of the fire that burned, uniting all the clans as one people, and of the Twisted Hair of old who walked the land.

A young man asked, "What has this to do with the stranger?"

With shining eyes, she looked at the man. "In the days when the Turtle People came, the Nunne'hi took our mother town and many of the wise Keetoowah, into their world under the mountain. There, the wisdom keepers hold the knowledge of the ancestors. The great Twisted Hair left the world to go into the hidden village. When he is most needed, it is said he will come to us with word from the keepers of wisdom within the holy place."

Twisted Hair thanked the old woman for remembering a story most had forgotten, then waited while the crowd filled out with the new arrivals. When they fell silent and expectant, he spoke. His voice carried far beyond the fire.

"Listen closely, for I will not come again while you are in the world. It is for you to remember my words, and see that they are made known to all, for they are the stories or our people. As long as they are told, we will live.

The story I bring you tonight is known by only a few, but it must be told to many, for within it is the secret that must be made known if human beings are to remain in this world. I have returned to tell you of things yet to come."

He heard someone say, "What is he, some kind of preacher?"

He raised his hand for silence, "Long ago I came to this place. The museum was not here then, or highways and buildings. There was only a village where a man named Kanagwa'ti lived. In that day, I brought a story of the Great Teacher of Peace, who came to the northlands many generations ago when only our people lived on this continent. In that day, he told of a time when a great white serpent would come. A great red snake would go out to meet him. The two serpents would begin a battle that would go on for many seasons. The white snake would gain size, strength and power. The red snake would become smaller and weaker. In time, only the white snake would stand. The red snake would lie upon the ground, his spirit gone from him. His people would wander lifeless in the land, as if they were dead but still walked.

You have heard this story many times, and you know who the two serpents are. For many generations, our people have walked this land as if there was no spirit in them. Some were ashamed of their blood and became more like the strangers than their own people. Many of the sacred ways of the ancestors have been abandoned and the land where their bones lie is torn by the machines of the white snake's children.

Long ago, I stood in the place where we now stand, and spoke to the Ani'yun-Wiya who lived here. I gave them the words of the great teacher of peace who told of the two serpents, and of the promise of the day when the life spirit would return to their descendants. I spoke of a sign that would mark the return of life and hope to our people. The sign was not for their day, but for their children's children. The promise was for you.

You have heard it said, look to the eagle, for you will see her fly her highest in the night, and she will not stop until she sits on the moon. When this sign is seen, it will mark the return of life to the people of our blood. When the eagle has landed, the red snake will arise.

You have seen the sign of the eagle. On the night you heard the words, *'Tranquility base here, the eagle has landed,'* that prophecy was fulfilled. The eagle flew her highest in the night and sat upon the moon. That is when the spirit of life came to rest once again in the hearts of our people. It is time to come alive and claim your place in the land. Take up the guardianship given to you by the Great One, for you are the keepers of the Earth.

The prophecies tell of great harm that will come upon the world, and it has already begun. I have been away from you for a long time, but others like me have traveled the land, holding wisdom in the mortal world. One who walks among you for many years will soon finish his journey and came home. His sadness has been great, for his eyes have witnessed the falling away of our people. He has walked among his own who showed him no honor, and only the children heard his story. It has been his joy to see the eagle land on the moon and watch the awakening of life in our people.

In clothing, hair and speech, you now show pride in a heritage that some of our people have forgotten. Where once the laws of the strangers forbade you to hold festivals and honor the above beings as our ancestors did, you remember the old ways.

The awakening has begun, and you are ready to hear prophecies that are given to you and your children, for I have come to prepare you for the time to come. Before we speak of things that are yet to be, it is the way of our people to recall the time of the beginning."

The people listened while he brought to their memory the story of the first human beings and the three shakings of their island world. He spoke of how all the people of the broken island were scattered to the four doors of the world. He reminded them of the great stone of wisdom and prophecy, and of the guardianship given to the people of the four doors.

"The people of the northern door were given the guardianship of fire. Their fire nature has caused them to spread and consume. In this, they serve the guardianship and bring together the family of human beings. In the work of their hands, they honor the fire. In all their works, you can see the fire, and it serves to bring human beings from the four doors of the world to know each other again, as they did in the beginning when all people lived together.

We are told we must learn to live as one human family, and close the circle of the four doors, or the shaking of the world will begin. The Great One has spoken many warnings and given dreams and visions to mark the approach of the time of purification, and now all the human family must hear his words. There are stories that have been told many times, but only within our own circles. Now it is time to tell them openly to any who will listen, for if the world is to stand, all must hear."

The circle around the fire was now filled. People stood in the field beyond, listening, and they all heard clearly. No sound broke the stillness. Even the children listened in silence.

"In the beginning, the world was shaken apart by three great wars. When the first people could not come together as brothers and sisters in one family of human beings, the world on which they lived was torn apart. Their story is kept in our memory as a warning, for we must do what they could not. As the Great One designed, we are all to live as one people.

Two times the Earth has shaken. Twice, we have heard the thunder and heeded the warning, but it is said that the third time, we stand alone. On the third shaking, only human beings can prevent the world from shaking apart. If harmony among the human family is not restored, you will tear apart the world, and the earth will be purified of the wrongs of man.

Long before the first shaking, you were warned by those who saw visions and dreams. You have heard of the vision of the little bug that traveled the land on a black ribbon. Human beings moved about the land because of the little bug. This was the first warning from the Great One.

"When the little bug flew from the black ribbon and took to the sky, the wise ones knew the people of the four doors of the world must come together and speak of peace. But the circle of the four doors was not closed. The people of the four sacred colors of the human family did not meet to talk of peace.

The first shaking of the world began.

You have seen the little bug. Even now it travels on a ribbon of highway and has brought you to this place. When it took to the sky, the wrath of the Great One sounded throughout the four doors of the world. The earth shook. Death and sorrow filled all the land as had not been since the beginning.

In the time of the first shaking, the elders warned that the circle of the four doors must be closed, that all the human beings of the earth must come together and talk of peace or the second shaking would come. This would bring even greater harm for the great gourd of ashes would be cast from the little bug in the sky and fall upon the earth. Where it fell, people would wither and die like blades of grass in the fire. Poison from the great gourd of ashes would spread afar, causing all in its path to sicken and die. The evil it brought to the Earth would never be rubbed out.

You have seen the first shaking of the world, and still the circle is not closed. You have seen the second shaking. The gourd of ashes has fallen and still the circle of the four doors has not closed. The four sacred colors of the human family have not joined as one family.

The keepers of wisdom watched as the warning of the first shaking was forgotten. The second shaking has come and gone, and still there is hatred among the family of human beings. They spoke of the warriors in the sky who dropped the gourd of ashes upon the land. The nation who dropped it must be warned, for in the third shaking, it will fall upon its makers.

Visions showed other signs of the approach of the third shaking. A House of Mica was seen, built in a great city in the east. It rose higher than the tallest tree and gleamed in the sun as if made of mica. It those days, the one who saw it did not know of glass. He saw that representatives from all the people of the four doors were to come together in that great house and talk of peace. If this came to past before the last sign, harmony would be restored, and humans would live as brothers and sisters as the Great One wanted. If it didn't take place, then the third and final shaking would come, and Earth would purify herself.

When the United Nations Building rose above the tallest trees, with walls of glass gleaming in the sun, the elders heard it was a place for all people to talk of peace. They said, 'Ahhh, the House of Mica.'

They watched as people from the Northern door, the Eastern door, and the Southern door came to sit in council together and talk of peace. But your people of the Western door were not among them. The circle of the four doors was not closed.

They talked of this, and of the prophecies that said they must knock four times on the door of the House of Mica and ask to speak. If at the time of the last sign, and after the forth knocking, the people of the red door were still outside the circle, the third shaking would come.

It is well known among you that a delegation, assembled from different tribes and Nations of the Native People of this land, traveled to The House of Mica and knocked upon the door. They said. 'We represent the indigenous people of this continent and we ask to be heard.' They were turned away and went back to their homes. The circle of the four doors was not closed when they knocked the first time.

Wise men and women of our blood talked of this, and of the signs of things to come. The prophecies spoke of a time when human beings would learn the plan of life and create new living things. They would change animals that already lived into something different than Creator made them. They would say, 'This is good,' and would release these new living beings upon the earth.

Some would warn against these beings, but their creators would say, 'They do good and not harm.' In the time of their children's children, these creatures will bring great trouble.

Other visions showed a time when the water would be poison and cause the fish to die. Clean water to drink would be scarce. The life would go out of the soil, leaving it weak and unable to produce enough food. Trees would begin to die when they were young, and from the tops down, not from the roots up as is nature's way for an old tree.

It was said that seeds and plants would be changed until they no longer brought forth grain and fruit, or that the fruit and grain they bore could not be eaten. Even the three sisters, corn, beans and squash, would be barren. Their seeds would not bring forth new fruit to nourish the people.

New sicknesses would come and bring death. Old sickness would return with greater power. Strange things were foretold that caused wonder even to the holy people. It was said that a great web would spread around the world and unite human beings from the four corners of the Earth. We have watched as the telegraph, then the telephone came, and now the web is here, and human beings are connected.

Keepers of wisdom watched as one after another the visions have come to past. We knew when delegates from the red door knocked upon the door of the house of Mica and asked to speak. Three times they knocked, and three times they were turned away. The last sign before the third shaking was at hand. They must knock the fourth time for if it appeared before the circle was closed, the purification would begin, and none could stop it.

Long ago, a dreamer saw a time when human beings would build a house and cast it into the sky. People from all the lands would rise up and live in the house in the sky. This was the final omen, for if the people of the red door were not welcomed in to the House of Mica when the house in the sky was completed, the beginning of sorrows would come.

It was foretold that we would look into the sky and see the stars in a different place, as if they had shifted from their path to the other side of the world. Lands that were once cold would be warm and warm places would see cold and ice. Many animals would leave the world for there would be no place for them. The balance between the animals and human beings would be disturbed and the natural order would be no more.

Visions showed a great city. There were houses, so tall that when you stood among them you could not see the sky. At sunrise, they were there, but by midday, there would be nothing left of the tall houses but smoke rising from ashes.

When you see this come to pass, know you have seen and heard the first thunder of the third shaking of the world.

The wisest among you have seen many of these signs and know their meaning. You have spoken of how all the people of the four doors must come together in the House of Mica and talk of peace. You have watched the people of the white door, the yellow door and black door find a place in the council circle, but the people of the red door have not. Three times they knocked and three times they were turned away.

When your people heard that a space station would soon be in the sky, and people of many lands would live there, the elders knew, they must knock again for the fourth and last time. This time, refusal meant it would be time to warn the people to go to the high mountains where perhaps a few would survive."

He opened the newspaper he held folded in his hand and gave it to the old woman who called him Twisted Hair. The woman opened it and read the date, December 1996, the year that just ended. On the first page she saw pictures of people she recognized. Native people, speaking before the leaders of all the nations of the world. She passed the paper around, so they could see once again a story that gave them great pride.

Twisted Hair repeated the story from memory.

"On November 22, and 23, 1993, delegations from the Algonquin, Lakota, Hopi, Iroquois, Mik-maq, Huichol, and Mayan Nations, spoke before the United Nations and delivered messages handed down through the generations of our people. They spoke of prophecies that warned of what is to come if we do not listen. Their message was: 'We must stand together, the four sacred colors of man, as the one family that we are, in the interest of peace. We must raise up leaders of peace and unite the religions of the world as a spiritual force strong enough to prevail in peace.'"

The newspaper passed from the circle, on to the crowd that had gathered in the field. Twisted Hair raised his voice, so all could hear.

"It is for you to remember what has been foretold. You live in the shadow of the third shaking of the world. The guardianship of Earth is given you, and her fate is in your hands. Your young will see changes you cannot understand, for if the world stands, it will be made new. Human Beings will change. The four sacred colors will unite, and a race of golden people will come into the world. Great truths will fall, and greater ones arise, but you must remember. The one truth lives within the stories you hold in your heart. All wisdom is hidden in the core of legend and the wise will find it. Keep them always, for they are your hope."

A man from the North held the newspaper up and read of how representatives of the Iroquois Nation met in New York's Central Park. There they held a ceremonial planting of a symbolic Tree of Peace. He spoke of the Great Teacher of Peace who came to his people long ago and told its story.

"Yes, there is hope in the stories of our ancestors," he said.

The old woman asked, "Can you tell us where to find the mother town? I long to stand on the mound where the sacred fire burned."

"Look to the ancestors," Twisted Hair said. "They will show you where it stood."

The crowd around the fire talked about what their elders told them about the mother town. They were familiar with many prophecies, for grandparents believed, but the young thought of other things. They drifted away, leaving the elders to discuss Twisted Hair's stories.

He listened long enough to know they understood. No one noticed when he walked away from the circle.

Two Nunne'hi women waited in the shadows at the edge of the ceremonial ground to guide him home. He followed, for he did not wish to linger in the strange land he once loved. The shape of the mountains had not changed, but too many houses cluttered every space and an unfamiliar smell hung in the air.

A few stars shown dimly in the sky, but far fewer than he remembered. He listened for the voices of night birds but all he heard was the dull roar of the little bugs as they traveled the ribbon of highway.

He followed the two Nunne'hi women back to the mother town under the mountain, to the woman who waited for him. Sha-cona-gee was no longer home.

Sope Returns to the Mountain.

Just to the North of the city of Atlanta Georgia, a creek flows past ruins of an old mill, built on the site where a little village once stood. Beside its banks, a worn-down mound of stone protects the bones of a woman who died of grief long ago. Now, the creek winds past big houses and highways. Golfers at the Atlanta Country Club can hear it rushing by on quiet mornings. It flows beneath a busy modern bridge, on to the wooden covered bridge at Concord, and beyond. They call it Sope Creek, and say it is named for an old Indian man who came to wander its banks, back before the Country Club or the covered bridge or the paper mill were built.

A few scattered farms stood along the creek then, after the Indians who used to live there were gone. Children who grew up on those farms said an old man came and told them stories. They described him as ancient, with long white hair worn twisted into ropes and bound with strips of leather. His clothing was strange, made of leather and beads, but worn and old.

The parents never saw the old man, but they listened when their children told his stories. They must have believed in him, because they gave the creek the name the children called the storyteller. Sope Creek, they called it, and it is still known by that name.

People who lived along the creek heard of him and wondered who he was. Some said he must have been a ghost, for surely there were no Indians around in those days. They had all had been taken away.

A mixed blood man told Sope's story and showed them a carved staff he claimed belonged to him.

The man insisted Sope was real and wrote stories of how he traveled along the creek long ago, before there were farm houses, when there were still Indians around and their villages stood along its banks. He tended a mound of stone he claimed marked the grave of Sope's mother. Sope camped beside it when he came to tell his stories.

When the Indian people were taken from their homes, marched away to the west, or to shallow graves along the trail, he said the old Indian storyteller returned to the place he once called home, to tell his tales to the children who came to live on their land. He felt safe with the children.

Old Sope listened from the shadows while the man held the staff and told stories about him. He was no more than a legend now, like the Twisted Hair, Tsi-s-qua, and the storytellers before them. He must trust his stories to the man for his time was done. He turned his face to the north to begin his final journey.

Tired and lonely, he trudged a no-longer-familiar trail, staying close to the forests, sleeping at night under the moon, waiting to cross bridges and highways until no one was there to see. He had no fear of the strangers. They were at home in the land that once belonged to his people and meant him no harm. He kept to himself because all his stories were told, and he had no wish to speak.

The world had changed since his last journey. Houses lined the road across the last mountain.

Down a cool path, still carpeted with pine needles, he walked. The mound that once stood tall in the mother town was worn down to no more than a low hill. Corn grew where the sacred fire once burned.

He set a course for the sacred mountain, seeking the outcropping that marked the entry to the mother town. Even though trees and vines obscured it, he knew where it stood.

Did he hear a faint cry?

"He is coming."

The scent of smoke from cooking fires wafted through the breeze.

The cry grew louder. "The storyteller is coming"

He caught sight of them through the trees, three men waiting at the foot of the mound. One of them so familiar his heart ached with the joy of reunion. Another, more legend than man, stood beside him, lifting his hand in welcome. The Nunne'hi who sent him on his journey, waited with them. Their voices called out to him and he broke into a run. With each step, he grew stronger.

Years of loneliness slipped away. He heard the music of dancing water and remembered when creeks still ran clear, the mountains were green and cool, and storytellers were met with joy as they drew near a town. The cries became a song.

"He is coming. Sope, the storyteller, is coming home."

The council house appeared through the foliage. Green hills rose beyond a clear, sweet river. Sweet fragrance of sage and cedar mingled with honeysuckle greeted him, and voices called his name. Tsi-s-qua embraced him. Twisted Hair welcomed him to the land inside the mountain, and the Nunne'hi led Old Sope inside.

His journey was over. He was home with a wealth of stories from the world outside to add to the store of knowledge held for the people.

Away in the lowlands, another storyteller lived in a fine house beside the creek, telling stories about the secret town in the Nunne'hi's mountain.

Sope told of books that recounted their stories to a generation that almost believed, and the spirit in the words that made them dream.

A few still listened to the dreams and learned true wisdom.

Inside the mountain, the storytellers, the Keetoowah, and the Nunne'hi, wait for the next storyteller to come home.

Donadagohvi
Wado.

Author's note
In the beginning.

The way the elders told it to me: in the days before the white people came, the wise Keetoowah lived in the mother town in the bend of a river. They knew the ways of healing, the wisdom of the stars, and the history of the Cherokee. They built the town 10,000 years ago and made a mound in its center. Atop the mound, they built a seven-sided lodge with places for all the seven clans to sit in council. A sacred fire burned there, representing the life that went out into the world from the Creator of all things. It held the spirit of our people and was the mother of all the seven fires that burned in the council houses of the seven clans.

In the time when winter faded into spring, came the festival of the new fires. Trusting that the sacred fire in the mother town would always be alive, the people doused their fires and came to rekindle them from the one sacred flame. Day and night, it burned, down through the centuries, sometimes banked in the coals that came to life the next day, sometimes burning low, sometimes leaping high to celebrate the unity and harmony of the people.

When the white people came, many things were lost. They say the mother town was probably taken then, when they came in great numbers to take what they desired. Fertile land beside a river would have been a great prize. All evidence of what it used to be would disappear under their towns and homes.

Some of the old people remembered a story of a great holy man who came to warn of the arrival of the Turtle

People the prophecies predicted. They say the holy man disappeared with the town. My grandpa suspected they were together.

I don't remember who told me the part of the story that came to my mind when the location of the mother town was found.

"The ancestors will come back and show us where it is."

I never expected the dead to return and point to that sacred place, but there is great truth in the improbable stories our grandparents told us. It happened just that way. Ancient bones were discovered in the ground, and the archaeologists came. They determined that a town once stood there in the bend of the Tuckaseegee River, a town where people lived for 10,000 years.

The years and the plow wore down the mound in the middle of what was now a cornfield, but when you learned what it used to be, you knew.

The site now belongs to the Eastern Band of Cherokee Indians and will be protected and honored. The young people came with red clay for the top of the mound to signify the fire that once burned there.

I went there to walk and remember the stories that were a treasured part of my childhood. First, I went to water in the Tuckaseegee, seven times under, each time with a prayer of thanksgiving that my mother was Cherokee, and the blood of those who once lived there flowed through my veins. I asked that my life would honor the best of the traditions and that Creator would bless the people who kept them alive.

Then I wrapped in a blanket and went to sit on the mound. I had a beeswax candle in a little handmade pot with me. I set it down atop the red clay the young people brought. I lit the candle and watched it burn while I remembered all my elders who had walked on, leaving only their stories. My grandfather, who told of hardships that followed the removal, of his grandfather who came back from the west and made his home in the Smoky Mountains. My grandmother who sent us to gather herbs to make medicines for our ills, the way her grandmother taught her. I remembered the people in Graham County who left an indelible memory of the language, spoken as it was long ago, and the sorrow and joy of being Cherokee.

Like the clans did in the old days, I took a spark of the fire from the sacred fire with me when I picked up the candle and went home. When it burned low, I lit another from it, and the fire still burns in my house and heart.

Today, I live near Sope Creek. I walk there and remember the stories of an old Indian who used to tell stories to the children who played there. I walked there recently and discovered an ancient stacked stone chimney hidden among the trees, the only remnants of a house that used to stand there.

I once found a mossy mound of stone under an oak tree beside the creek, and wondered what, or who lay beneath it.

The greatest gift a writer has is the ability to take those bits of the past, those morsels of reality, and turn them into a story that honors that fleeting moment when it all fades into legend.

GLOSSARY

Ani Waya: Wolf People. People of the Wolf Clan, one of the seven clans of the Cherokee, or the Wolves themselves. Believed to be the guard dogs and hunters of Kenati, the first man.

Asi: The sweat lodge. Often used as winter sleeping quarters in cold weather. It was a low circular structure of logs covered with earth. The fire smoldering within it kept it warm.

Awi Usdi: The mythic chief of the deer tribe. He is described as snow white, about the size of a medium dog, with a large rack of antlers. He has always been friendly and helpful to humans, but his first duty is to his own people, the deer. He allows hunters to take a reasonable number of deer, if the appropriate ceremonies are kept, and punishes with sickness, any who kill more than they need or forget the rituals.

Dakwa: A mythic great fish. In modern usage it is the name of the whale.

Galun-lati: Above or on high. The Cherokee overworld. The first home of the Cherokee. Many of the mythic beings have returned there and no longer live on the earth. Some, like Awi Usdi visit earth to care for their people here. The Uktena now lives there for he is too dangerous for the earth. Since death is of a very temporary nature there, little harm is done even if he does kill someone. The Cherokee version of heaven.

Ghigham: A title sometimes used for the Beloved Women, who were women with a great deal of authority in Cherokee society. They were known by other titles, such as War Women, or Pretty Women. In old times they often earned the title in battle. A recent Beloved Woman was Maggie Wachacha, a Snowbird Cherokee who served as a council scribe and translated proceedings into the Cherokee syllabary for many years. A joint council of the Eastern Band and the Cherokee Nation designated her and Lula Gloyn of the Qualla boundary, as Beloved Women in 1984. They earned the title based on long years of service to their people, a reputation for wisdom and gentleness, and their role in maintaining the history, knowledge and traditions of the people. The custom continues with Myrtle Driver is a beloved Woman today.

Raven Mocker: Ka'lanu-Ahyeli'ski. A kind of witch in Cherokee mythology. They were shape changers who could take on the form of a large raven and fly through the air. You could tell them from real ravens by their size and the fact that fire sparks would come from their wings as they flew. They were among the most feared of the witches because they could become invisible, enter the home of a sick, wounded, or old person, and take their heart without leaving a scar or any sign. The victim would die, and as soon as the raven mocker ate the heart, he would have the life which was left to the victim. In this way they lived many years more than mortals, and could live indefinitely as long as hearts were available.

Nunne'hi: [nun-ya'-hee] An invisible race of Cherokee. They were full sized people, very handsome and richly dressed. They usually lived in places where others wouldn't choose to live, such as bald mountains or old mounds. Cherokee people have told stories of having been lost and rescued by the Nunne'hi. They say they were taken to their homes, which were beautiful with rich fertile corn fields, and were well fed and entertained. When taken outside the village and directed to the path home, they looked back and could see no sign of the Nunne'hi town. Some say that time was different in the Nunne'hi villages and what seemed like a single day there could be weeks, months or even years in the real world. There are numerous stories of Nunne'hi warriors intervening to assist the Cherokee in battle.

Tsali: A Cherokee hero. Revered by his people for sacrificing his life and the lives of his sons to save the remnants of the people who were hiding out in the hills to avoid removal to the west. An historical marker honoring him is at the Swain County Courthouse in Bryson City North Carolina, for it is on that spot that Tsali and his sons were executed by firing squad.

Uktena: A mythical monstrous serpent who in the old days lived in the Smoky Mountains. He was large enough to coil around a mountain with his head resting on the crest. He had an enormous appetite and often fed on humans. There was great power in his scales and to own even one gave a holy person or conjuror magical abilities, especially prophecy. At the top of the Uktena's head was the great talismanic crystal, Ulunsu ti. The Uktena had to be slain to obtain it but it was the most powerful talisman known.

Unehlanuhi: Creator. Also the name the Cherokee call the Sun.